Programming ArcGIS Pro with Python

Automate your ArcGIS Pro geoprocessing tasks with Python.

Eric Pimpler

Geospatial Training Services
215 W Bandera #114-104
Boerne, TX 78006
PH: 210-260-4992
Email: sales@geospatialtraining.com
http://geospatialtraining.com
Twitter: @gistraining

About the Author

Eric Pimpler is the founder and owner of Geospatial Training Services (geospatialtraining. com) and have over 25 years of experience implementing and teaching GIS solutions using Esri software. Currently he focuses on ArcGIS Pro and Desktop scripting with Python and the development of custom ArcGIS Enterprise (Server) and ArcGIS Online web and mobile applications with JavaScript.

Eric is the also the author of several other books including *Programming ArcGIS with Python Cookbook* (https://www.packtpub.com/application-development/programming-arcgis-python-cookbook-second-edition), *Spatial Analytics with ArcGIS* (https://www.packtpub.com/application-development/spatial-analytics-arcgis), *Building Web and Mobile ArcGIS Server Applications with JavaScript* (https://www.packtpub.com/application-development/building-web-and-mobile-arcgis-server-applications-javascript), and *ArcGIS Blueprints* (https://www.packtpub.com/application-development/arcgis-blueprints).

If you need consulting assistance with your ArcGIS Pro project please contact Eric at eric@geospatialtraining.com or sales@geospatialtraining.com. Geospatial Training Services provides contract application development and programming expertise for ArcGIS Pro, ArcGIS Desktop, ArcGIS Enterprise (Server), and ArcGIS Online using Python, .NET/ArcObjects, and JavaScript.

Downloading and Installing Exercise Data for this Book

Before beginning any of the exercises in this book you will want to download and install the exercise data. Please follow these instructions to download and install the exercise data.

1. Open a web browser and download the dataset from either:

   - Dropbox -https://www.dropbox.com/s/5l5glsmq1gbo7f1/ProgrammingPro. zip?dl=0

   - Amazon - http://s3.amazonaws.com/VirtualGISClassroom/ IntroProgrammingArcGISProPython/ProgrammingPro.zip

2. Using Windows Explorer or File Explorer create a c:\Student folder on your computer.

3. Unzip the downloaded exercise data to the c:\Student folder

4. The final folder structure should be c:\Student\ProgrammingPro. There will be a number of subfolders under ProgrammingPro.

Table of Contents

## Chapter 1

Fundamentals of the Python Language

Python supports many of the programming constructs found in other languages. In this chapter, we'll cover many of the basic language features found in Python. Initially, we'll delve into language features, such as adding comments to your code, importing modules, creating and assigning data to variables, and using the built-in primitive data types such as strings and numbers.

Next, we'll look at the more complex data types that Python offers, such as lists, tuples, and dictionaries. Classes and objects are a fundamental concept in object-oriented programming and in the Python language. We'll introduce you to these complex data structures, which you'll use extensively when you write geoprocessing scripts with ArcGIS Pro.

In addition to this, we'll cover statements, including decision support and looping structures to make decisions in your code, and/or looping through a code block multiple times along with the `with` statement, which is used extensively with the new `cursor` objects from the `arcpy` data access module (`arcpy.da`) that are used to insert, search, and update data.. By the end of this chapter, you will have learned the following:

- Commenting code
- Importing modules
- Creating variables
- Using built-in data types (strings, numbers, lists, dictionaries)
- Manipulating strings
- Using classes and objects
- Decision support statements
- Looping structures
- Handling errors with try/except
- Using functions
- Working with files

Python Language Fundamentals

To effectively write geoprocessing scripts for ArcGIS Pro, you are going to need to understand at least the basic features of the Python language. Python is easier to learn than most other programming languages, but it does take some time to learn and effectively use. This section will teach you how to create variables, assign various data types to variables, understand the different types of data that can be assigned to variables, use different types of statements, work with objects, read and write files, and import Python modules.

Commenting Code

Python scripts should follow a common structure. It is a commonly accepted practice that the beginning of each script should serve as documentation, detailing the script name, author, and a general description of the processing provided by the script. This introductory documentation will help you and other programmers in the future to quickly scan the details and purpose of a script. This documentation is accomplished in Python through the use of comments. Comments are lines of code that you add to your script that serve as documentation of what functionality the script provides. These lines of code begin with a single pound sign (#) or a double pound sign (##), and are followed by whatever text you need to document the code. The Python interpreter does not execute these lines of code. They are simply used to document your code. In the code example below, the commented lines of code are displayed with a single pound sign that prefixes the line of code. You should also strive to include comments throughout your script to describe important sections of your script. This will be useful to you (or another programmer) when the time comes to update your scripts.

```
# This script programmatically adds layers to an ArcGIS Project
# Author: Eric Pimpler
# Last Editied: 10/01/2017
import arcpy.mp as map
try:
    aprx = map.ArcGISProject("CURRENT")
    for m in aprx.listMaps("Map"):
        for lyr in m.listLayers():
            if lyr.name == "Zoning":
                m.removeLayer(lyr)
```

```
#lyr = map.LayerFile(r"C:\Student\Zoning.lyrx")
#m.addLayer(lyr)
#m.addBasemap("Imagery")
#m.addDataFromPath(r"C:\Student\
Trippville_GIS.gdb\Floodplains")

    except Exception as e:
        print("Error: " + e.args[0])
```

Importing Modules

Although Python includes many built-in functions, you will frequently need to access specific bundles of functionality, which are stored in external modules. For instance, the Math module stores specific functions related to processing numeric values and the os module provides functionality for working with files and folders at the operating system level. Modules are imported through the use of an import statement. When writing geoprocessing scripts with ArcGIS, you will always need to import the arcpy module, which is the Python package that is used to access GIS tools and functions provided by ArcGIS. The import statements will be the first lines of code (not including comments) in your scripts. The following lines of code import the arcpy and os modules. The Python os module provides a way of interfacing with the underlying operating system:

```
import arcpy
import os
```

Variables

At a high level, you can think of a variable as an area in your computer's memory that is reserved to store values while the script is running. Variables that you define in Python are given a name and a value. Different areas of your script can then access the values assigned to variables, simply by referring to the variable name. For example, you might create a variable that contains a feature class name, which is then used by the Buffer tool to create a new output dataset. To create a variable, simply give it a name followed by the assignment operator, which is just an equal sign (=), and then a value:

```
fcParcels = "Parcels"
fcStreets = "Streets"
```

The following table illustrates the variable name and values assigned to the variable using the preceding code example:

Variable name	Variable value
fcParcels	Parcels
fcStreets	Streets

There are certain naming rules that you must follow when creating variables, including the following:

- It can contain letters, numbers, and underscores
- The first character must be a letter or underscore
- No special characters can be used in a variable name other an underscore
- Python keywords and spaces are not permitted

There are a few dozen Python keywords that must be avoided, including class, if, for, while, and others. These keywords are typically highlighted in a different font color from other Python statements.

Here are some examples of legal variable names in Python:

- featureClassParcel
- fieldPopulation
- field2
- ssn
- my_name

These are some examples of illegal variable names in Python:

- class (Python keyword)
- return (Python keyword)
- $featureClass (illegal character, must start with a letter)
- 2fields (must start with a letter)
- parcels&Streets (illegal character)

Python is a case-sensitive language, so pay particular attention to the capitalization and naming of variables in your scripts. Case-sensitivity issues are probably the most common source of errors for new Python programmers, so always consider this as a possibility when you encounter errors in your code. Let's look at an example. The following is a list of three variables; note that although each variable name is the same, the casing is different, resulting in three distinct variables.

- mapsize = "22x34"
- MapSize = "8x11"
- Mapsize = "36x48"

If you print these variables, you will get the following output:

```
print mapsize
>>> 22x34

print MapSize
>>> 8x11   #output from print statement

print Mapsize
>>>36x48   #output from print statement
```

Python variable names need to be consistent throughout the script. The best practice is to use camel casing, wherein the first word of a variable name is all lowercase and then each successive word begins with an uppercase letter. This concept is illustrated in the following example with the fieldOwnerName variable name. The first word (field) is all lowercase followed by an uppercase letter for the second word (Owner) and third word (Name):

```
fieldOwnerName
```

In Python, variables are dynamically typed. **Dynamic typing** means that you can define a variable and assign data to it without specifically defining that a variable name will contain a specific type of data. Commonly used data types that can be assigned to variables include the following:

We will discuss each of these data types in greater detail in the coming sections.

Data type	Example value	Code example
String	"Streets"	fcName = "Streets"
Number	3.14	percChange = 3.14
Boolean	True	ftrChanged = True
List	"Streets", "Parcels", "Streams"	lstFC = ["Streets", "Parcels", "Streams"]
Dictionary	'0':Streets,'1':Parcels	dictFC = {'0':Streets,'1':Parcels]
Object	Extent	spatialExt = map.extent

In other languages like C#, you would need to define a variable's name and type before using it. This is not necessary in Python. To use a variable, simply give it a name and value, and you can begin using it right away. Python does the work behind the scenes to figure out what type of data is being held in the variable.

In the following C# code example, we've created a new variable called aTouchdown, which is defined as an integer variable, meaning that it can contain only integer data. We then assign the 6 value to the variable:

```
int aTouchdown;
aTouchdown = 6;
```

In Python, this variable can be created and assigned data through dynamic typing. The Python interpreter is tasked with dynamically figuring out what type of data is assigned to the variable:

```
aTouchdown = 6
```

There may be times when you know that your script will need a variable, but don't necessarily know ahead of time what data will be assigned to the variable. In these cases, you could simply define a variable without assigning data to it. Here, you will find a code example that depicts creating a variable without assigning data:

```
aVariable = ''
aVariable = None
```

Data that is assigned to the variable can also be changed while the script is running.

Variables can hold many different kinds of data, including primitive data types, such as strings and numbers along with more complex data, such as lists, dictionaries, and even objects. We're going to examine the different types of data that can be assigned to a variable along with various functions that are provided by Python to manipulate the data.

Built-in Data Types

Python has a number of built-in data types. The first built-in type that we will discuss is the string data type. We've already seen several examples of string variables, but these types of variables can be manipulated in a lot of ways, so let's take a closer look at this data type.

Strings

A string is an ordered collection of characters that store and represent text-based information. This is a rather dry way of saying that string variables hold text. String variables are surrounded by single or double quotes when assigned to a variable. Examples could include a name, feature class name, a Where clause, or anything else that can be encoded as text. The code examples below illustrate the creation of variables that have been defined as a string data type.

```
myName = "Eric"
mySSN = "467-35-3567"
myAge = "21"
featureClassName = 'Roads'
polyCentroid = '-95.4567, 34.6468'
```

String manipulation

Strings can be manipulated in a number of ways in Python. String concatenation is one of the more commonly used functions and is simple to accomplish. The + operator is used with string variables on either side of the operator to produce a new string variable that ties the two string variables together:

```
shpStreets = "c:\\GISData\\Streets" + ".shp"
print(shpStreets)
```

Running this code example produces the following result:

```
>>>c:\\GISData\\Streets.shp
```

String equality can be tested using Python's == operator, which is simply two equal signs placed together. Don't confuse the equality operator with the assignment operator, which is a single equal to sign. The equality operator tests two variables for equality, while the assignment operator assigns a value to a variable:

```
firstName = "Eric"
lastName = "Pimpler"
firstName == lastname
```

Running this code example produces the following result because the firstName and lastName variables are not equal:

```
>>>False
```

Strings can be tested for containment using the in operator, which returns True if the first operand is contained in the second:

```
fcName = "Floodplain.shp"
print(".shp" in fcName)
>>>True
```

I have briefly mentioned that strings are an ordered collection of characters. What does this mean? It simply means that we can access individual characters or a series of characters from the string and that the order of the characters will remain the same until we change them. In Python, this is referred to as **indexing** in the case of accessing an individual character, and **slicing** in the case of accessing a series of characters.

Characters in a string are obtained by providing the numeric offset contained within square brackets after a string. For example, you could obtain the first string character in the fc variable by using the fc[0] syntax. Python is a zero-based language, meaning the first item in a list is 0. Negative offsets can be used to search backwards from the end of a string. In this case, the last character in a string is stored at the -1 index. Indexing always creates a new variable to hold the character:

```
fc = "Floodplain.shp"
print(fc[0])
>>>'F'
print(fc[10])
>>>'.'
print(fc[13])
>>>'p'
```

The following image illustrates how strings are an ordered collection of characters with the first character occupying the **0** position, the second character occupying the **1** position, and each successive character occupying the next index number:

Each character is also assigned a negative integer that allows you to read the string from right to left in addition to reading from left to right.

While string indexing allows you to obtain a single character from a `string` variable, string slicing enables you to extract a contiguous sequence of strings. The format and syntax is similar to indexing, but with the addition of a second offset, which is used to tell Python which characters to return.

The following code example provides an example of string slicing. The `theString` variable has been assigned a value of `Floodplain.shp`. To obtain a sliced variable with the contents of `Flood`, you would use the `theString[0:5]` syntax:

```
theString = "Floodplain.shp"
print(theString[0:5])
>>>Flood
```

Python slicing returns the characters beginning with the first offset up to, but not including, the second offset. This can be particularly confusing for new Python programmers and is a common source of errors. In our example, the returned variable will contain the `Flood` characters. The first character, which occupies the `0` position, is `F`. The last character returned is the character occupying the fourth (`4`) index, which corresponds to the `d` character. Notice that the character at index position `5` is not included since Python slicing only returns characters up to, but not including, the second offset

Either of the offsets can be left off. This, in effect, creates a wild card. In the case of `theString[1:]`, you are telling Python to return all characters starting from the second character to the end of the string. In the second case, `theString[:-1]`, you are telling Python to start at character zero and return all characters except the last.

Python is an excellent language to manipulate strings and there are many additional functions that you can use to process this type of data. Most of these are beyond the scope of this text, but in general, all the following string manipulation functions are available:

- String length
- Casing functions for conversion to upper and lowercase
- Removal of leading and trailing whitespace
- Finding a character within a string
- Replacement of text
- Splitting into a list of words based on a delimiter
- Formatting

Paths to Datasets

Your Python geoprocessing scripts for ArcGIS Pro will often need to reference the location of a dataset on your computer or, perhaps, a shared server. References to these datasets will often consist of paths stored in a variable. In Python, pathnames are a special case that deserves some extra mention.

The backslash character in Python is a reserved escape character and a line continuation character, thus there is a need to define paths using two back slashes, a single forward slash, or a regular single backslash prefixed with `r`. These pathnames are always stored as strings in Python. You'll see an example of this in the following section.

The path in the code below could cause some problems in Python because when the interpreter encounters a single backslash it interprets it as a command. For example, a `\t` in Python is a command to insert a tab and `\n` is a command to insert a new line. There are a number of such "commands" in Python. Python doesn't interpret the single backslash as a path to a file so you have to handle paths to files using one of a variety of methods.

```
fcParcels = "c:\Data\Parcels.shp"
```

You can handle paths to file and folders using any of the three methods seen below:

```
fcParcels = "c:/Data/Parcels.shp"
fcParcels = "c:\\Data\\Parcels.shp"
fcParcels = r"c:\Data\Parcels.shp"
```

I would recommend that you use the final method shown here that continues to use a single backslash as a divider between folders and files, but with the addition of a lowercase r (raw) to indicate to the Python interpreter that it should interpret backslashes as a path rather than a command.

String formatting

String formatting in Python provides a more advanced way to combine string-processing tasks. It allows you to perform multiple type specific substitutions on a string in a single step. String formatting is not required in any circumstance, but rather provides a convenience mechanism. There are two types of string formatting currently in use: string formatting expressions and string formatting methods calls. We'll examine both in more detail in this section.

String formatting expressions

String formatting expressions follow the format below:

'Place a 6 inch pipe parallel to the main'

The left hand side of the expression is the string to be formatted and the right hand side of the expression is the data that will be inserted into the string. A percent sign is used as the divider between the expression on the left and the data on the right. In this example, `'Place a %i inch pipe parallel to the %s'` is the string to be formatted. Inside the string are two placeholders: `%i` and `%s`. These are simply placeholders where data will be inserted. In the case of `%i` an integer value, 6 in this case, will be inserted at this location. The string `'main'` will be inserted at the `%s` placeholder. A number of characters can be inserted after the percent sign. Some of the most common include the following:

> %s – String
> %i – Integer
> %d – Decimal

The right hand side of the expression is the data that will be inserted into the string to be formatted. In this case the data is hard coded, but in most cases this will be data that has been pulled from a data source such as a feature class, table, or file.

The end result will be the string value: 'Place a 6 inch pipe parallel to the main'. Keep in mind that string formatting is not required. You could create variables to hold the contents of the pipe size and pipe type. However, the use of string formatting is more convenient in many ways, and reduces the amount of code you have to write to accomplish the same thing.

String formatting method

The string formatting method accomplishes the same thing as a string formatting expression, but the syntax differs. Take a look at the example below. The string format method is used in this case. Two parameters are passed into the method: `'Indian Wells'`, and `3050`. These values will be inserted into the corresponding index position bounded by curly braces inside the string to be formatted.

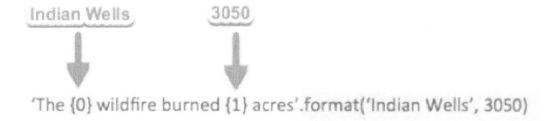

Indian Wells   3050

'The {0} wildfire burned {1} acres'.format('Indian Wells', 3050)

The Indian Wells wildfire burned 3050 acres

The end result will be the string `'The Indian Wells wildfire burned 3050 acres'`. Again, keep in mind that it is not required that you use either the string formatting method or expression. It is possible to accomplish the same result using variables, but it's certainly more efficient from a coding perspective to use the formatting method or expression.

Numbers

Python also has built-in support for numeric data, including `int`, `long`, `float`, and `complex` values. Numbers are assigned to variables in much the same way as strings, with the exception that you do not enclose the value in quotes and obviously, it must be a numeric value.

Python supports all the commonly used numeric operators, including addition, subtraction, multiplication, division, and modulus or remainder. In addition to this, functions used to return the absolute value, conversion of strings to numeric data types, and rounding are also available.

Although Python provides a few built-in mathematical functions, the `math` module can be used to access a wide variety of more advanced `math` functions. To use these functions, you must specifically import the `math` module as follows:

```
import math
```

Functions provided by the `math` module include those that return the ceiling and floor of a number, the absolute value, trigonometric functions, logarithmic functions, angular conversion, and hyperbolic functions.

Lists

A third built-in data type provided by Python is list. A list is an ordered collection of elements that can hold any type of data supported by Python as well as being able to hold multiple data types at the same time. This could be numbers, strings, other lists, dictionaries, or objects. So, for instance, a list variable could hold numeric and string data at the same time. Lists are zero-based, with the first element in the list occupying the **0** position. This is illustrated here:

listOfValues = ['streets', 'mains', 'parcels', 'valves']

Each successive object in the list is incremented by one. Additionally, lists have the special capability of dynamically growing and shrinking.

Assigning a series of values enclosed by brackets creates a list. To pull a value from a list, simply use an integer value in brackets along with the variable name. The following code example provides an illustration of this.

```
fcList = ["Hydrants", "Water Mains", "Valves", "Wells"]
fc = fcList[0] ##first item in the list - Hydrants
print(fc)
>>>Hydrants
fc = fcList[3]  ##fourth item in the list - Wells
print(fc)
>>>Wells
```

You can add a new item to an existing list by using the append() method, as seen in this code example:

```
fcList.append("Sewer Pipes")
print(fcList)
>> Hydrants, Water Mains, Valves, Wells, Sewer Pipes
```

You can also use slicing with lists to return multiple values. To slice a list, you can provide two offset values separated by a colon, as seen in the following code example. The first offset indicates the starting index number and the second indicates the stopping point. The second index number will not be returned. Slicing a list always returns a new list:

```
fcList = ["Hydrants", "Water Mains", "Valves", "Wells"]
fc = fcList[0:2] ##get the first two items — Hydrants, Water
Mains
```

Lists are dynamic in nature, meaning that you can add and remove items from an existing list as well as change the existing contents. This is all done without the need to create a new copy of the list. Changing values in a list can be accomplished either through indexing or slicing. Indexing allows you to change a single value, while slicing allows you to change multiple list items.

Lists have a number of methods that allow you to manipulate the values that are part of the list. You can sort the contents of the list in either an ascending or descending order through the use of the sort() method. Items can be added to a list with the append() method, which adds an object to the end of the list, and with the insert() method, which inserts an object at a position within the list. Items can be removed from a list with the `remove()` method, which removes the first occurrence of a value from the list, or the `pop()` method, which removes and returns the object at the end of the list. The contents of the list can also be reversed with the `reverse()` method.

List comprehension

List comprehension in Python provides a concise method for creating lists. It combines a `for` loop with list creation. The syntax for list comprehension is written inside square brackets because they are used to create new lists. While not required, list comprehension often runs much faster than separating the `for` loop from the list creation. The code examples below illustrate the difference between using list comprehension and not. The result is the same, but list comprehension requires fewer lines of code and creates the list faster.

List created through list comprehension

```
L = [1,2,3,4,5]
y = [x + 10 for x in L]
```

List created using traditional method

```
L = [1, 2, 3, 4, 5]
for i in L:
    L[i] += 10
```

The two screenshots below further illustrate the basic form of list comprehension along with a more advanced form of list comprehension that uses a filter.

Tuples

Tuples are similar to lists but with some important differences. Just like lists, tuples contain a sequence of values. The contents of a tuple can include any type of data just like lists. However, unlike lists, the contents of a tuple are static. After a tuple has been created, you can't make any changes to the sequence of the values nor can you add or remove values. This can be a good thing for situations where you want data to always occupy a specific position. Creating a tuple is as simple as placing a number of comma-separated values inside parentheses, as shown in the following code example:

```
fcTuples = ("Hydrants", "Water Mains", "Valves", "Wells")
```

You've probably noticed that creating a tuple is very similar to creating a list. The only difference is the use of parentheses instead of square braces around the values.

Similar to lists, tuple indices start with an index value of 0. Access to values stored in a tuple occurs in the same way as lists. This is illustrated in the following code example:

```
fcTuples = ("Hydrants", "Water Mains", "Valves", "Wells")
print fcTuples[1]
>>>Water Mains
```

Tuples are typically used in place of a list when it is important for the contents of the structure to be static. You can't ensure this with a list, but you can with a tuple. Currently, the only time tuples are used in `arcpy` is through the data access (`arcpy.da`) module when working with cursor objects. Cursor objects, as you'll discover in *Chapter 9: Using the Arcpy Data Access Module*, use tuples when returning attribute values and geometry from a feature class or table.

Dictionaries

Dictionaries are another type of collection object in Python. They are similar to lists, except that dictionaries are an unordered collection of objects. Instead of fetching objects from the collection through the use of an offset, items in a dictionary are stored and fetched by a key. Each key in a dictionary has an associated value, as seen here:

dFires = { 'FireName' : 'Bastrop', 'Acres' : 3000, 'Contain' : 'N', 'Location' : (-95.456, 32.948) }

In the example above, `FireName`, `Acres`, `Contain`, and `Location`. Each of these keys has an associated value. For example, `Bastrop` is the value associated with `FireName` and `3000` is the value associated with `Acres`. Referencing the key retrieves the values. It's very similar to using a traditional dictionary wherein you look up a word and it provides a definition for the word.

Similar to lists, dictionaries can grow and shrink in place through the use of methods on `dictionary`. In the following code example, you will learn to create and populate a `dictionary` and see how values can be accessed through the use of a key. Dictionaries are created with the use of curly braces. Inside these braces, a colon follows each key and then a value is associated with the key. Commas separate these key/value pairs:

```
##create the dictionary
dictLayers = {'Roads': 0, 'Airports': 1, 'Rail': 2}

##access the dictionary by key
print(dictLayers['Airports'])
>>>1
print(dictLayers['Rail'])
>>>2
```

Basic `dictionary` operations include getting the number of items in a dictionary, acquiring a value using a key, determining if the key exists, converting the keys to a list, and getting a list of values. The `dictionary` objects can be changed, expanded, and shrunk in place. What this means is that Python does not have to create a new `dictionary` object to hold the altered version of the dictionary. Stating the key value in brackets and setting it equal to some value can accomplish assigning values to a dictionary key.

Unlike lists, dictionaries can't be sliced due to the fact that their contents are unordered. Should you have the need to iterate over all the values in a dictionary, simply use the `keys()` method, which returns a collection of all the keys in the dictionary and can then be used individually to set or get their value.

Classes and Objects

Classes and objects are a fundamental concept in object-oriented programming. While Python is more of a procedural language, it also supports object-oriented programming. In object-oriented programming, classes are used to create object instances. You can think of classes as blueprints for the creation of one or more objects. Each object instance has the same properties and methods, but the data contained in an object can differ. Objects are complex data types in Python composed of properties and methods, and can be assigned to variables just like any other data type. Properties contain data associated with an object, while methods are actions that an object can perform.

These concepts are best illustrated with an example. In arcpy, the extent class is a rectangle that represents the envelope of a geographic feature and is specified by providing the coordinate of the lower-left corner and the coordinate of the upper-right corner in map units. The extent class contains a number of properties and methods. Properties include XMin, XMax, YMin, YMax, spatialReference, and others. The minimum and maximum of x and y properties provide the coordinates for the extent rectangle. The spatialReference property holds a reference to a spatialReference object for extent. Object instances of the extent class can be used both to set and get the values of these properties through dot notation. An example of this is seen in the following code example:

```
# get the extent of the county boundary
ext = row[0].extent
# print out the bounding coordinates and spatial reference
print("XMin: " + str(ext.XMin))
print("XMax: " + str(ext.XMax))
print("YMin: " + str(ext.YMin))
print("YMax: " + str(ext.YMax))
print("Spatial Reference: " + ext.spatialReference.name)
```

Running this script yields the following output:

```
XMin: 2977896.74002
XMax: 3230651.20622
YMin: 9981999.27708
YMax:10200100.7854
Spatial Reference:
NAD_1983_StatePlane_Texas_Central_FIPS_4203_Feet
```

The `extent` class also has a number of methods, which are actions that an object can perform. In the case of this particular object, most of the methods are related to performing some sort of geometric test between the `extent` object and another geometry. Examples include `contains()`, `crosses()`, `disjoint()`, `equals()`, `overlaps()`, `touches()`, and `within()`.

One additional object-oriented concept that you need to understand is **dot notation**. Dot notation provides a way of accessing the properties and methods of an object. It is used to indicate that a property or method belongs to a particular class.

The syntax for using dot notation includes an object instance followed by a dot and then the property or method. The syntax is the same regardless of whether you're accessing a property or a method. A parenthesis and zero or more parameters at the end of the word following the dot indicates that a method is being accessed. Here are a couple of examples to better illustrate this concept:

```
Access a Property: extent.XMin
Access a Method: extent.touches()
```

Statements

Each line of code that you write with Python is known as a **statement**. There are many different kinds of statements, including those that create and assign data to variables, decision support statements that branch your code based on a test, looping statements that execute a code block multiple times, and others. There are various rules that your code will need to follow as you create the statements that are part of your script. You've already encountered one type of statement: variable creation and assignment.

Statement Indentation

Statement indentation deserves a special mention, as it is critical to the way Python interprets code. Compound statements in Python use indentation to create a group of statements. This includes the `if`/`then`, `for`, `while`, `try`, and `with` statements, all of which we'll discuss in the upcoming sections. The Python interpreter uses indentation to detect these code blocks.

The beginning of a compound statement is defined through the use of a colon. All lines following the beginning of the compound statement should be indented the same distance.

You can use any number of spaces to define the indentation, but you should use the same indentation level for each statement. A common practice is to define indentation through the use of a tab. When the Python interpreter encounters a line that is less indented, it will assume that the code block has ended.

The following code block illustrates this concept through the use of a `try` statement. Notice that there is a colon after the `try` statement. This indicates that the statements that follow are part of a compound statement and should be indented. These statements will form a code block. Also, an `if` statement is inside the `try` statement. This too is a compound statement as defined by the colon at the end of the statement. Therefore, any statements that are part of the `if` statement should be further indented. You should also notice that there is a statement that is not indented inside the `if` statement, but is at the same level. This `statement4` is part of the `try` code block but not part of the `if` code block that immediately precedes it:

```
try:
    if <statement1>
        <statement2>
        <statement3>
    <statement4>
    <..........>
except:
    <statement>
    <..........>
except:
    <statement>
    <..........>
```

Many languages, including JavaScript, Java, and .NET, use curly braces to indicate a group of statements. Python uses indentation instead of curly braces in an attempt to cut down on the amount of code you have to write and make code more readable. Anyone who has ever used these other languages can attest to the difficulty in reading code that contains many curly braces. However, indentation does take some getting used to and is critical to the way that Python executes lines of code.

Print Statement

The `print()` function in Python is used to send output to the shell window, and is typically used to output error messages or progress information to the shell window while the script is running. In Python 2.x the use of parentheses are optional. In other words, it can be called as an expression or a function. So, either of the following statements are acceptable in Python 2.x.

```
print "Hello World"
print("Hello World")
```

However, keep in mind that ArcGIS Pro uses Python 3.x exclusively, and in this version of the language `print()` is a function and requires the use of parentheses.

print("Hello World")

Decision Support Statement

The `if/elif/else` statement is the primary decision-making statement in Python and tests for a `true/false` condition. Decision statements enable you to control the flow of your programs. Here are some example decisions that you can make in your code: if the variable holds a point feature class, get the X, Y coordinates; if the feature class name equals `Roads`, then get the contents of the `Name` field.

Decision statements, such as `if/elif/else`, test for a `true/false` condition. In Python, a `true` value means any nonzero number or nonempty object. A `false` value indicates *not true* and is represented in Python with a zero number or empty object. Comparison tests return values of one or zero (true or false). Boolean and/or operators return a true or false operand value:

```
if fcName == 'Roads':
    arcpy.Buffer_analysis(fc, "c:\\temp\\roads.shp", 100)
elif fcName == 'Rail':
    arcpy.Buffer_analysis(fc, "c:\\temp\\rail.shp", 50)
else:
    print("Can't buffer this layer")
```

Python code must follow certain syntax rules. Statements execute one after another until your code branches. Branching typically occurs through the use of `if/elif/else`. In addition to this, the use of looping structures, such as `for` and `while`, can alter the statement flow. Python automatically detects statement and block boundaries, so there is no need for braces or delimiters around your blocks of code. Instead, indentation is used to group statements in a block. Also, many languages terminate statements with the use of a semicolon, but Python simply uses the end of line character to mark the end of a statement. Compound statements include a ":" character. Compound statements follow the pattern, that is, header terminated by a colon. Blocks of code are then written as individual statements and are indented underneath the header.

As mentioned previously, Python detects a contiguous section of code through the use of indentation. By default, all Python statements should be left justified until looping, decision support, try/except, and with statements are used. This includes for and while loops, if/else statements, try/except statements, and with statements. All statements indented the same distance belong to the same block of code until a line that is less indented ends this block.

Looping statements

Looping statements allow your program to repeat lines of code over and over as necessary. A while loop repeatedly executes a block of statements as long as the test at the top of the loop evaluates to true. When the condition test evaluates to false, Python begins interpreting code immediately after the while loop.

In the next code example, a value of 10 has been assigned to the x variable. The test for the while loop then checks to see if x is less than 100. If x is less than 100, the current value of x is printed to the screen and the value of x is incremented by 10. Processing then continues with the while loop test. The second time, the value of x will be 20; so the test evaluates to true once again. This process continues until x is equal to 100. At this time, the test will evaluate to false and processing will stop.

It is very important that while statements have some way of breaking out of the loop. Otherwise, you will wind up in an infinite loop. An infinite loop is a sequence of instructions in a computer program that loops endlessly, either due to the loop having no terminating condition, having one that can never be met, or one that causes the loop to start over:

```
x = 10
while x < 100:
    print(x)
    x = x + 10
```

A `for` loop executes a block of statements a predetermined number of times. They come in two varieties—a counted loop to run a block of code a set number of times, and a list loop that enables you to loop through all the objects in a list. List loops are far more commonly used due to the extensive use of `list` objects in Python. The syntax of a for list loop is as follows:

```
for <target> in <object>:
    <statements>
```

Example

```
listLayers = ['Hydrants', 'Mains', 'Valves']
for layer in listLayers:
    print layer.name
```

layer is a dynamic variable

The object in this case is a Python `list`, while the target is a dynamic variable. As a programmer you simply need to name the variable. The `for` loop will handle the assignment of values to the variable. Items in the list are assigned to the target, one by one during execution of the loop.

The following code example illustrates the use of a `for` list loop. After creation, the `list` is passed into the `for` loop along with a variable named `layer`. Inside the for loop will be one or more lines of code that perform some sort of processing.

```
listLayers = ["Hydrants", "Mains", "Valves"]
for layer in listLayers:
    print(layer.name)
```

There are times when it will be necessary for you to break out of the execution of a loop. The `break` and `continue` statements can be used to do this. The `break` jumps out of the closest enclosing loop, while `continue` jumps back to the top of the closest enclosing loop. These statements can appear anywhere inside the block of code.

Try statements

A `try` statement is a compound statement that is used to handle errors (exceptions) in your code. Exceptions are a high-level control device used primarily for error interception or triggering.

Exceptions in Python can either be intercepted or triggered. When an error condition occurs in your code, Python automatically triggers an exception, which may or may not be handled by your code. It is up to you as a programmer to catch an automatically triggered exception.

Exceptions can also be triggered manually by your code. In this case, you would also need to provide an exception handling routine to catch these manually triggered exceptions.

There are two basic types of `try` statements: `try/except/else` and `try/finally`. The basic `try` statement starts with a `try` header line followed by a block of indented statements. Then, this is followed by one or more optional `except` clauses that name the exceptions that are to be caught.

```
import arcpy
import sys

inFeatureClass = arcpy.GetParameterAsText(0)
outFeatureClass = arcpy.GetParameterAsText(1)

try:
    # If the output feature class exists, raise an error

    if arcpy.Exists(inFeatureClass):
        raise overwriteError(outFeatureClass)
    else:
        # Additional processing steps
        print("Additional processing steps")
except overwriteError as e:
    # Use message ID 12, and provide the output feature class
    # to complete the message.

    arcpy.AddIDMessage("Error", 12, str(e))
```

The `try`/`except`/`else` statement works as follows. Once inside a `try` statement, Python marks the fact that you are in a `try` block and knows that any exception condition that occurs at this point will be sent to the various `except` statements for handling.

If an error occurs, processing will stop and an `Exception` object will be generated and then passed to the exception handlers. If a matching exception is found, the code block inside the `except` block is executed.

If no exception conditions occur in the `try` block, the code pointer will then jump to the `else` statement and execute the code block contained by the `else` statement before moving to the next line of code that follows the `try` block.

The other type of `try` statement is the `try`/`finally` statement, which allows for finalization actions. When a `finally` clause is used in a `try` statement, its block of statements always run at the very end, whether an error condition occurs or not.

Here is how the `try`/`finally` statement works: if an exception occurs, Python runs the `try` block, then the `except` block, followed by the `finally` block, and then execution continues past the entire `try` statement.

If an exception does not occur during execution, Python runs the `try` block, then the `finally` block. This is useful when you want to make sure an action happens after the code block runs, regardless of whether an error condition occurs. Cleanup operations, such as closing a file or a connection to a database, are commonly placed inside a `finally` block to ensure that they are executed regardless of whether an exception occurs in your code:

```python
import arcpy

try:
    if arcpy.CheckExtension("3D") == "Available":
        arcpy.CheckOutExtension("3D")
    else:
        # Raise a custom exception
        raise LicenseError

    arcpy.env.workspace = "D:/GrosMorne"
    arcpy.HillShade_3d("WesternBrook", "westbrook_hill", 300)
    arcpy.Aspect_3d("WesternBrook", "westbrook_aspect")
except LicenseError:
    print("3D Analyst license is unavailable")
```

```
except:
    print(arcpy.GetMessages(2))
finally:
    # Check in the 3D Analyst extension
    arcpy.CheckInExtension("3D")
```

The with statement

The `with` statement is handy when you have two related operations that need to be executed as a pair with a block of code in between. A common scenario is to use `with` statements is opening, reading, and closing a file. Opening and closing a file are the related operations, and reading a file and doing something with the contents is the block of code in between. When writing geoprocessing scripts with ArcGIS Pro, the `cursor` objects are ideal for the `with` statements.

We'll discuss the `cursor` objects in great detail in a later chapter, but I'll briefly describe these objects now. Cursors are an in-memory copy of records from the attribute table of a feature class or table. There are various types of cursors. Insert cursors allow you to insert new records, search cursors are a read-only copy of records, and update cursors allow you to edit or delete records. Cursor objects are opened, processed in some way, and closed automatically using a `with` statement.

The closure of a file or cursor object is handled automatically by the `with` statement, resulting in cleaner, more efficient coding. It's basically like using a `try`/`finally` block, but with fewer lines of code. In the following code example, the `with` block is used to create a new search cursor, read information from the cursor, and implicitly close the cursor:

```
import arcpy

fc = "c:/data/city.gdb/streets"

# For each row print the Object ID field, and use the SHAPE@AREA
# token to access geometry properties

with arcpy.da.SearchCursor(fc, ("OID@", "SHAPE@AREA")) as cursor:
    for row in cursor:
        print("Feature {0} has an area of {1}".format(row[0],
        row[1]))
```

Functions

A function is a named group of statements that are executed together and serve two primary roles: code reuse and dividing a task into smaller sections. All functions have a name, can be passed parameters, and can (but don't have to) return a value. Take a look at the simple function below and then we'll discuss the syntax of functions.

```python
def unique_values(table, field):
    data = arcpy.da.TableToNumPyArray(table, [field])
    return numpy.unique(data[field])
```

The `def` statement in Python is used to define the contents of a function. Each function is given a name, which in this case is `unique_values`. Function naming follows the same rules as variable naming. Give your functions descriptive names, and start them with letters or an underscore.

Functions always have a pair of parentheses at the end of the name, and may or may not accept arguments. Arguments, also called parameters, are values that are passed to a function. In the example above, `table` and `field` are the arguments. These values become local variables inside the function. Any additional variables that are created inside a function are local to that function and can't be accessed outside the function.

A function is a compound statement so the definition of a function always ends with a colon and the contents of the function are indented. The contents of a function include any number of lines of code that execute together as a group. A `return` statement can be used to return a value to the caller of the function.

File input and output

You will often find it necessary to retrieve or write information to files on your computer. Python has a built-in object type that provides a way to access files for many tasks. We're only going to cover a small subset of the file manipulation functionality provided, but we'll touch on the most commonly used functions, including opening and closing files, and reading and writing data to a file.

Python's `open()` function creates a file object, which serves as a link to a file residing on your computer. You must call the `open()` function on a file before reading and/or writing data to a file. The first parameter for the `open()` function is a path to the file you'd like to open. The second parameter corresponds to a mode, which is typically read (r), write (w), or append (a). A value of r indicates that you'd like to open the file for read-only operations, while a value of w indicates you'd like to open the file for write operations. In the event that you open a file that already exists for write operations, this will overwrite any data currently in the file, so you must be careful with the write mode. The append mode (a) will open a file for write operations, but instead of overwriting any existing data, it will append the new data to the end of the file. The following code example shows the use of the open() function to open a text file in a read-only mode:

```
with open('Wildfires.txt','r') as f:
```

Notice that we have also used the with keyword to open the file, ensuring that the file resource will be *cleaned up* after the code that uses it has finished executing.

After a file has been opened, data can be read from it in a number of ways and using various methods. The most typical scenario would be to read data one line at a time from a file through the readline() method. The readline() function can be used to read the file one line at a time into a string variable. You would need to create a looping mechanism in your Python code to read the entire file line by line. If you would prefer to read the entire file into a variable, you can use the read() method, which will read the file up to the **end of file (EOF)** marker. You can also use the readlines() method to read the entire contents of a file, separating each line into individual strings, until the EOF is found.

In the following code example, we have opened a text file called Wildfires.txt in read-only mode and used the readlines() method on the file to read its entire contents into a variable called lstFires, which is a Python list containing each line of the file as a separate string value in the list. In this case, the Wildfire.txt file is a comma-delimited text file containing the latitude and longitude of the file along with the confidence values for each file. We then loop through each line of text in lstFires and use the split() function to extract the values based on a comma as the delimiter, including the latitude, longitude, and confidence values. The latitude and longitude values are used to create a new Point object, which is then inserted into the feature class using an insert cursor:

```
import arcpy, os
try:

    arcpy.env.workspace = "C:/data/WildlandFires.mdb"
    # open the file to read
```

```
with open('Wildfires.txt','r') as f:    #open the file
    lstFires = f.readlines() #read the file into a list
    cur = arcpy.InsertCursor("FireIncidents")

    for fire in lstFires: #loop through each line
        if 'Latitude' in fire: #skip the header
            continue
    vals = fire.split(",") #split the values based on comma
    latitude = float(vals[0]) #get latitude
    longitude = float(vals[1]) #get longitude
    confid = int(vals[2]) #get confidence value
    #create new Point and set values
    pnt = arcpy.Point(longitude,latitude)
    feat = cur.newRow()
    feat.shape = pnt
    feat.setValue("CONFIDENCEVALUE", confid)
    cur.insertRow(feat) #insert the row into featureclass
except:
    print(arcpy.GetMessages()) #print out any errors
finally:
    del cur
    f.close()
```

Just as is the case with reading files, there are a number of methods that you can use to write data to a file. The write() function is probably the easiest to use and takes a single string argument and writes it to a file. The writelines() function can be used to write the contents of a list structure to a file. In the following code example, we have created a list structure called fcList, which contains a list of feature classes. We can write this list to a file using the writelines() method:

```
outfile = open('c:\\temp\\data.txt','w')
fcList = ["Streams", "Roads", "Counties"]
outfile.writelines(fcList)
```

Summary

In this chapter, we covered some of the fundamental Python programming concepts that you'll need to understand before you can write effective geoprocessing scripts. We covered the basic language constructs, including importing modules, creating and assigning variables, if/else statements, looping statements, and the various data-types including strings, numbers, lists, dictionaries, and objects. You also learned how to read and write text files.

In the next chapter, you will learn the basic techniques used to write geoprocessing scripts for ArcGIS Pro with Python. You'll learn how to install and configure the PyCharm development environment, use the embedded Python window in ArcGIS Pro, import the `arcpy` module to your scripts, use variables to store data, and access the various `arcpy` modules.

Introduction to Using Arcpy
in ArcGIS Pro

In this chapter, we will cover the following topics:

- Installing and configuring PyCharm
- Creating your first ArcGIS Pro Python script
- Using the ArcGIS Pro Python Window

Arcpy is a Python library for ArcGIS Pro that enables you to automate your geoprocessing tasks, perform geographic data analysis, data conversion, data management, and much more. It also offers code completion and a rich set of reference documentation. Code completion is best illustrated by typing a keyword and then a dot and then a dropdown list of available choices appears, offering a set of choices from which you can make a selection. This makes you a faster more accurate programmer.

Arcpy consists of a core library along with several additional modules including the Mapping (mp), Data Access (da), Network Analyst (na), and Spatial Analyst (sa) modules illustrated below. These additional modules can be thought of as extensions to the primary arcpy module.

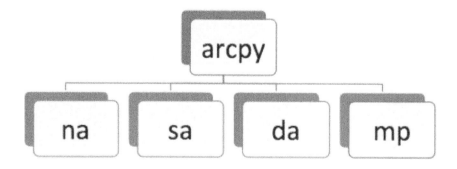

Introducing Conda

Python is the primary language for automating geoprocessing tasks in ArcGIS Pro and ArcGIS 10.x. It is a highly versatile and extensible language with many third party libraries that can be used alongside ArcGIS. This includes statistical, image processing, charting and graphing, and many others. Organizing and managing all these libraries can be difficult. ArcGIS Pro uses the **conda** package manager to install third party libraries, associate libraries with specific projects, and in general simplify the process of sharing tools.

You're probably going to see a number of different, but similar terms when reading about conda. So before we go any further let's discuss some of those terms so that you'll understand them. Conda, which is what ArcGIS Pro uses, is an open source package and environment management system. Conda includes the installation of a number of default packages.

ArcGIS Pro has it's own conda environment as you'll soon see. A conda environment is a set of Python packages that can be used in one or multiple projects. **Pip**, which is similar to conda, is also an open source package and environment management system. Many Python developers have used pip for many years, and if so you'll be glad to hear that pip can still be used from inside conda. **Anaconda** is a data science platform that has several hundred commonly used packages specifically for data science. It uses conda at the core. Finally, **Miniconda** is a minimal version of conda that doesn't include any installed packages by default.

There are literally thousands of pre-existing Python packages that can be used in your scripts alongside `arcpy`. Managing these packages, including installation and association with a particular project can be difficult. Conda serves as a package manager, installs third party Python libraries, associates libraries with specific projects, and in general simplifies the process of sharing tools. You'll become more familiar with the conda environment as we move through the book. Python scripts that use `arcpy` for geoprocessing scripts must be run from inside the conda environment. The ArcGIS Pro conda environment is called **arcgispro-py3**.

Adding Python packages using ArcGIS Pro

The **Project** tab in ArcGIS Pro includes a **Python** tab that allows you to access the **Python Package Manager**. Clicking the **Python** button displays a dialog including options for getting a list of installed packages, adding or updating packages, or deleting packages. This is illustrated in the screenshot below.

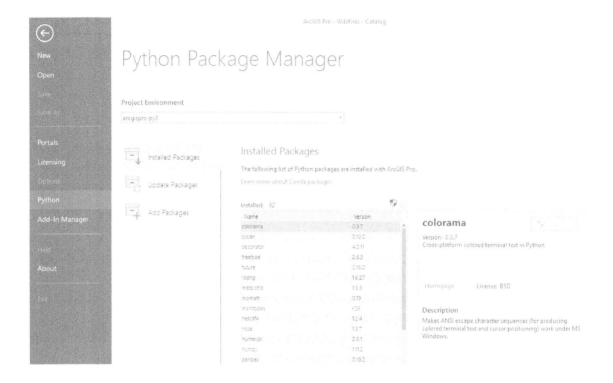

Development environments for Python scripts

There are many development environments that you can use to write Python scripts. ArcGIS Pro includes a **Python Window** that you can use to write and execute lines of code one line at a time. While the **Python Window** is not a bad place to begin learning about Python and how it can be used to automate your geoprocessing tasks, it's not the best development environment by any means. There are many Integrated Development Environments (IDE), that you can use to write, execute, and debug your scripts. Some of these IDEs include PyCharm, IDLE, Spyder, Wing, Visual Studio, and others. In this book we'll use the very popular PyCharm IDE for writing most of our scripts. You will need to configure PyCharm to use the ArcGIS Pro conda environment. You'll learn how to do that shortly.

ArcGIS Pro Python Window

ArcGIS Pro includes an embedded **Python Window** that you can use to write code and see immediate feedback. This tool provides a good learning environment for experimenting with arcpy and Python. It's probably not the best tool for long term programming efforts, but it does provide some advantages, particular for new programmers. The **Python Window** interacts directly with ArcGIS Pro and has access to all the layers and other contents of your map, environment settings, and other functionality. Arcpy, it's core modules, and core Python standard library is all included. You can execute a single command or entire scripts in the **Python Window**. Tools and functions can be entered, executed, and then easily recalled using the up and down arrow keys on your keyboard. Python code stored in an existing script can be loaded and executed, and finally the **Python Window** also provides auto-completion.

The screenshot below shows the **Python Window** as it appears in ArcGIS Pro. It is sectioned into two areas: Python prompt and transcript. The Python prompt is used to enter commands. To execute the command you simply click the **Enter** key on your keyboard. The output from your commands is written to the transcript area above.

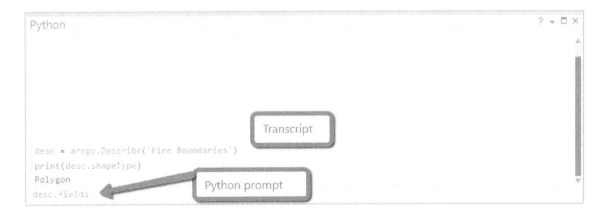

PyCharm

After downloading and installing PyCharm you'll need to do some configuration to tell it what environment to use, which is ArcGIS Pro in this case. You'll learn how to do this in just a few moments in the first exercise of the chapter. PyCharm includes a Community Edition, which is free, along with a licensed version. The Community Edition will probably work fine for most people. To configure PyCharm to use the ArcGIS Pro conda environment you will need to follow the setting presented in the upcoming exercise.

It is not required that you use PyCharm as your development environment for writing scripts for ArcGIS Pro. Other possibilities include Python Tools for Visual Studio, Wing IDE, and Spyder. Many of you may have used PyScripter in the past when developing geoprocessing scripts for ArcGIS Desktop. However, Pyscripter doesn't work well in virtual environments so at this time it can't be used with ArcGIS Pro running in a conda environment. Hopefully that will change at some point in the near future as PyScripter is a very popular IDE for GIS programmers using Python with ArcGIS Desktop.

Running Python Scripts

There are many ways that you can run a Python script. The **Python Window** in ArcGIS Pro can be used to write and execute lines of code one line at a time. While the **Python Window** is not a bad place to begin learning about Python and how it can be used to automate your geoprocessing tasks, it's not the best development environment by any means. As we've already discussed there are many development environments that can be used to write and execute your scripts as well. In addition, Python scripts can be run from the command prompt through a batch file called **propy.bat**, as scheduled tasks using the **Windows Task Scheduler**, and they can also be run when referenced through batch files.

You can use a batch file called propy.bat to execute a standalone Python script. This would serve as a replacement for calling **python.exe** from the command prompt. You might be asking yourself why this is necessary. With ArcGIS Pro, when building a project, you could create and use a conda environment with specific sets and versions of Python packages that are different than the default. Propy.bat will automatically determine the applications active conda environment and activate it to run a standalone script. The process followed when executing propy.bat with a script file includes activation of the ArcGIS Pro conda environment, starting Python, running the specified script, and exiting Python. You can see an example of this below.

```
C:\Program Files\ArcGIS Pro\bin\Python\scripts\propy.bat my_script.py
```

You don't have to use propy.bat to execute a Python script from the command prompt. You can instead continue to call **python.exe** and pass a script as the parameter to this call.

However, you'll want to make sure you call python.exe found in the ArcGIS Pro conda environment as seen below.

```
C:\Program Files\ArcGIS Pro\bin\Python\envs\arcgispro-py3\python.exe
```

Importing arcpy and arcpy modules

We covered the topic of importing libraries in *Chapter 1: Fundamentals of the Python Language*. In this section you'll learn more about importing the libraries specific to ArcGIS Pro.

Before you can use a Python library in your script it must first be imported. Importing a library is what gives you access to the classes and functions that are available in the library. To import arcpy you simply type import arcpy as the first line of code in your script.

```
import arcpy
```

After importing the arcpy library you will then be able to run any geoprocessing tool for which you have a license, and you can use the classes and functions that are part of arcpy. Remember that arcpy also includes several modules that contain additional classes and functions. To access these modules you'll need to import them with an import statement as seen in the code example below that imports the mapping module, known as arcpy.mp.

```
import arcpy.mp
```

You may not always want to import an entire library or module. For example, you may only need a single class from a library rather than the entire library. You can use the from-import-as structure in Python to accomplish this as seen in the code example below.

```
from arcpy import env as ENV
ENV.workspace = 'c:/data'
```

Exercise 1: Installing and configuring PyCharm

Getting ready

The PyCharm Integrated Development Environment (IDE) is a very popular tool for developing Python scripts. It certainly isn't the only tool that can be used with ArcGIS Pro, but it provides an advanced development environment that integrates well with ArcGIS Pro. We'll use PyCharm for most of the scripts in this class.

Python is the primary language for automating geoprocessing tasks in ArcGIS Pro. It is a highly versatile and extensible language with many third party libraries that can be used alongside ArcGIS Pro. There are literally thousands of pre-existing Python packages that can be used in your scripts alongside arcpy. Managing these packages, including installation and association with a particular project can be difficult, and conda can be used to manage this process. Python scripts that use Arcpy for geoprocessing scripts must be run from inside the conda environment.

How to do it...

Follow these steps to learn how to download, install, and configure PyCharm to work with the ArcGIS Pro conda environment:

Note: Before completing the exercises in this book you will need to download and install the exercise data. Please follow the directions below to download and install the exercise data. You will not be able to complete the exercises in this book until this is done.

Open a web browser and download the dataset from **either**:

Dropbox - https://www.dropbox.com/s/5l5glsmq1gbo7f1/ProgrammingPro.zip?dl=0

Amazon - http://s3.amazonaws.com/VirtualGISClassroom/IntroProgrammingArcGISProPython/ProgrammingPro.zip

Using Windows Explorer or File Explorer create a `c:\Student` folder on your computer.

Unzip the downloaded exercise data to the `c:\Student` folder

The final folder structure should be `c:\Student\ProgrammingPro`. There will be a number of subfolders under `ProgrammingPro`.

1. The ArcGIS Pro conda environment is called **arcgispro-py3**. Open Windows Explorer and navigate to `C:\Program Files\ArcGIS\Pro\bin\Python\envs\arcgispro-py3`. This is the conda environment for ArcGIS Pro. You'll use this path later when configuring PyCharm so make note of it. Inside this folder you'll see a series of folders and files that basically correspond to an installation of Python. The screenshot below illustrates what you should be seeing.
Note: If you installed ArcGIS Pro under your Windows login rather than for All Users the path will be somewhat different. The path will be `c:\Users\<username>\appdata\local\Programs\ArcGIS\Pro\bin\Python\envs\arcgispro-py3`.

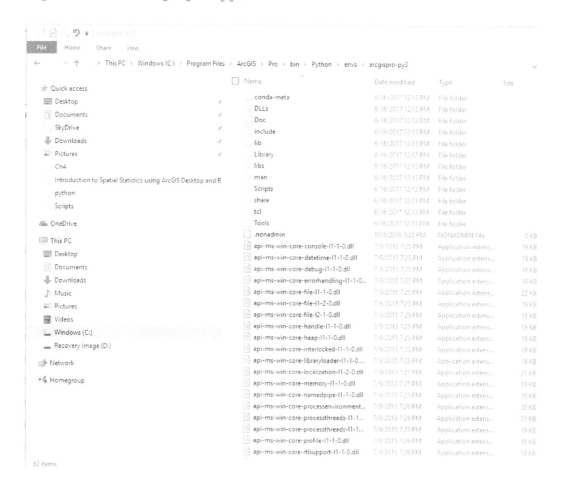

2. Now let's examine some of the Python packages that are installed with ArcGIS Pro and the conda environment. Open ArcGIS Pro and select any existing project that

you've created in the past or create a new project from one of the project templates provided by ArcGIS Pro.

3. After the project opens, click the Project tab in ArcGIS Pro, and then click the Python tab as seen in the screenshot below. This displays the Python Package Manager for ArcGIS Pro. It includes a list of all the packages that have already been installed with the ArcGIS Pro conda environment as well as options for updating existing packages or installing new packages. Take some time to examine some of the packages that have been installed.

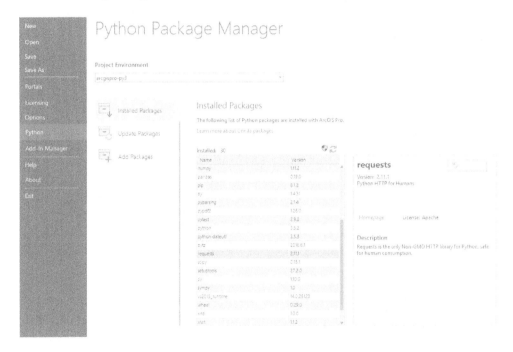

4. You can close ArcGIS Pro now.

5. Open a web browser and go to https://www.jetbrains.com/pycharm

6. Click the Download Now button.

7. Select the Community edition and click the Download button.

8. Double click the downloaded .exe file to begin the installation process.

9. Accept the defaults and make sure to check the box for Create Associations for .py files and optionally the Desktop shortcuts for the launchers as seen in the screenshot below.

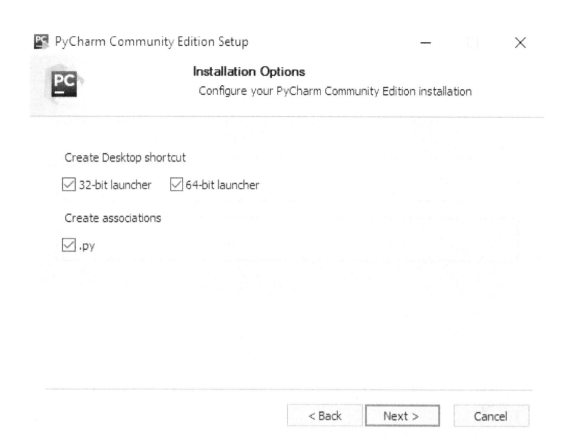

10. Start PyCharm.

11. The first time you start PyCharm you'll be prompted to import settings as seen in the screenshot below. You can just select Do not import settings and click OK.

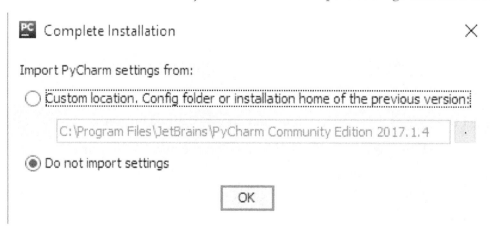

12. Accept any default values you see for the initial configuration.

13. Click Create New Project as seen in the screenshot below.

PyCharm Community Edition

Version 2017.1.4

☀ Create New Project

☞ Open

⬇ Check out from Version Control ▾

⚙ Configure ▾   Get Help ▾

14. You'll be prompted to select the location of the project along with the Interpreter to use. Define the following inputs.

- Location: `c:\Student\ProgrammingPro\Scripts`
- Interpreter: `c:\Program Files\ArcGIS\Pro\bin\Python\envs\arcgispro-py3\python.exe`

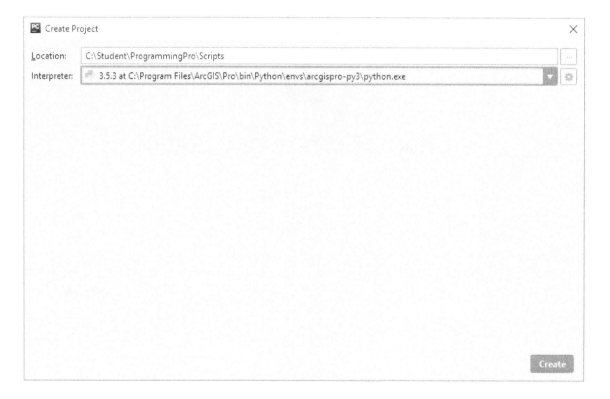

15. Click the Create button.

16. This will configure the current project to use the ArcGIS Pro conda environment, but you might prefer to have PyCharm use this environment for all new projects rather than having to set it each time. You can do this as well. In PyCharm select File | Default Settings.

17. Click Project Interpreter and set the Project Interpreter path to `c:\Program Files\ArcGIS\Pro\bin\Python\envs\arcgispro-py3\python.exe` as seen in the screenshot below.

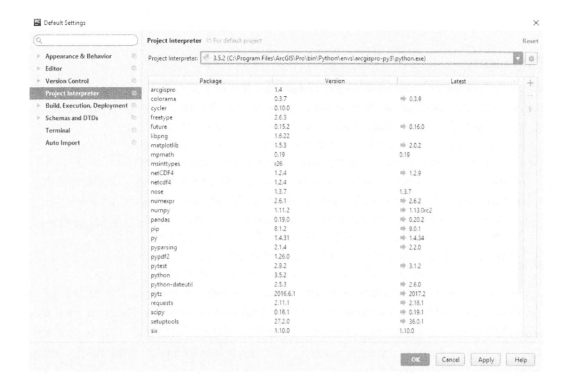

18. Click OK to apply the setting. Each new project that you create going forward will now use the ArcGIS Pro conda environment.

In conclusion...

In this exercise you learned more about the ArcGIS Pro conda environment, how to use ArcGIS Pro to view existing Python packages, update packages, and delete packages. You also learned how to install and configure PyCharm to use the ArcGIS Pro conda environment. In the next exercise you'll learn some fundamentals of using `arcpy`.

Exercise 2: Creating your first ArcGIS Pro script

Getting ready

In this exercise you'll learn some basic techniques that you'll use many times throughout the book. You'll work with both PyCharm and the ArcGIS Pro Python window to create and execute geoprocessing scripts.

Geoprocessing scripts that you write for ArcGIS Pro can be executed in a variety of environments, but all will need to adhere to a similar structure. In this exercise you'll learn the basic concepts of creating a script, importing modules, creating an error handling structure, performing geoprocessing, and running the script in different environments.

How to do it...

PyCharm, like ArcGIS Pro, operates around the concept of a project. In the last exercise you configured PyCharm to use the ArcGIS Pro conda environment. That only needs to be done one time so now when you create new projects in PyCharm they will automatically refer to this ArcGIS Pro conda environment. You also created a project in the first exercise so when you open PyCharm it should automatically load this project, which refers to `c:\ Student\ProgrammingPro\Scripts`.

Note: Before completing the exercises in this book you will need to download and install the exercise data. Please follow the directions below to download and install the exercise data. You will not be able to complete the exercises in this book until this is done.

Open a web browser and download the dataset from **either**:

Dropbox - https://www.dropbox.com/s/5l5glsmq1gbo7f1/ ProgrammingPro.zip?dl=0

Amazon - http://s3.amazonaws.com/VirtualGISClassroom/ IntroProgrammingArcGISProPython/ProgrammingPro.zip

Using Windows Explorer or File Explorer create a c:\Student folder on your computer.

Unzip the downloaded exercise data to the c:\Student folder

The final folder structure should be c:\Student\ProgrammingPro. There will be a number of subfolders under ProgrammingPro.

1. Open PyCharm

2. Your PyCharm environment should appear as seen in the screenshot below.

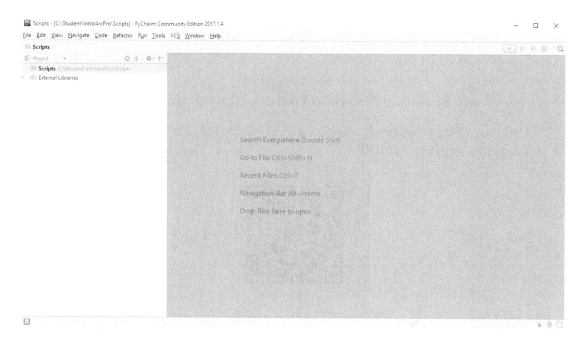

3. In PyCharm select **File | New | Python File**.

4. Name the file `MyFirstScript` and click **OK**.

5. In the script window import the `arcpy` package. This will be the first line of code you write in every script. It's what gives you access to the ArcGIS Pro library of functionality.

   ```
   import arcpy
   ```

6. Create a Python error handling structure to enable exception trapping and handling. The bulk of your code will go inside this `try` block.

   ```
   try:
   except Exception as e:
       print("Error: " + e.args[0])
   ```

7. Inside the `try` block (do not retype the try/except handler), get a reference to the current ArcGIS Pro project using the CURRENT keyword.

```
try:
    aprx = arcpy.mp.ArcGISProject("CURRENT")
except Exception as e:
    print("Error: " + e.args[0])
```

Note: You may have noticed that PyCharm includes code completion that allows you to select a property or function. This handy feature saves time and decreases errors due to typos. You can use the Tab or Enter key to select an item from the dropdown list to automatically complete the code.

8. Create a `for loop` that loops through all the maps in the project and for each map get a list of all the layers in the map and print out the names. We'll cover the details of this section of code in much more detail later in the book. Basically though the `ArcGISProject` object contains a `listMaps()` method that you can call to get a list of `Map` objects in a project. The `Map` object in turn, has a `listLayers()` method you can call to get a list of the layers in a specific `Map`.

```
try:
    aprx = arcpy.mp.ArcGISProject("CURRENT")
    for m in aprx.listMaps():
        print("Map: " + m.name)
        for lyr in m.listLayers():
            print("   " + lyr.name)
except Exception as e:
    print("Error: " + e.args[0])
```

9. Initially you're going to execute this script in the ArcGIS Pro Python window. Open ArcGIS Pro and load the `ArcGIS Pro − Ex2A.aprx` project found in the `c:\Student\ProgrammingPro\Chapter2` folder.

10. Click the **Analysis** tab and then the **Python window** tool to display the window seen in the screenshot below. The Python window is divided into two sections: transcript and Python prompt. The prompt, which is the small band at the very bottom of the window, is where you write code or load an existing Python script and the transcript section displays the output. The transcript section covers most of the area of the window.

11. Right click inside the Python prompt and select Load Code.

12. Navigate to the `c:\Student\ProgrammingPro\Scripts` folder and select `MyFirstScript.py` and click Open. The Python prompt should now appear as seen in the screenshot below.

```
import arcpy
try:
    aprx = arcpy.mp.ArcGISProject("CURRENT")
    for m in aprx.listMaps():
        print("Map: " + m.name)
        for lyr in m.listLayers():
            print("   " + lyr.name)
except Exception as e:
    print("Error: " + e.args[0])
```

13. Click the Enter key on your keyboard to execute the code. The results should be displayed as seen in the screenshot below. Note that the name of the Map has been displayed along with all the layers in the Map, which have been indented.

```
Python                                                               ? ▾ ☐ ✕


import arcpy
try:
    aprx = arcpy.mp.ArcGISProject("CURRENT")
    for m in aprx.listMaps():
        print("Map: " + m.name)
        for lyr in m.listLayers():
            print("   " + lyr.name)

except Exception as e:
    print("Error: " + e.args[0])
Map: Map
  Creeks and Streams
  Lakes and Ponds
  City Limits
  Parcels
  Topographic
```

14. Next we'll run this same script in PyCharm as a stand-alone script. Return to
    PyCharm and select Run | Run MyFirstScript. This time you'll get an error
    message as seen in the screenshot below. The question is why did you get this
    error? When you run a stand-alone script in a Python development environment,
    the operating system command line, or as a scheduled task, you can't use the
    CURRENT keyword when referencing an ArcGIS Pro project. Instead, you need to
    include the full path to the ArcGIS Pro project you want to reference.

```
"C:\Program Files\ArcGIS\Pro\bin\Python\envs\arcgispro-py3\python.exe" C:/Student/IntroArcPro/Scripts/MyFirstScript.py
Error: CURRENT

Process finished with exit code 0
```

15. Update the line of code that references the ArcGISProject object as seen below
    and re-run the script to see the output.

    ```
    aprx = arcpy.mp.ArcGISProject(r'c:\Student\ProgrammingPro\
    Chapter2\Ex 2A.aprx')
    ```

16. The output should now appear as seen in the screenshot below.

```
"C:\Program Files\ArcGIS\Pro\bin\Python\envs\arcgispro-py3\python.exe" C:/Student/IntroArcPro/Scripts/MyFirstScript.py
Map: Map
  Creeks and Streams
  Lakes and Ponds
  City Limits
  Parcels
  Topographic

Process finished with exit code 0
```

In conclusion…

In this exercise you learned some basic techniques for structuring your Python scripts, importing the `arcpy` Python package, generating a list of information in an ArcGIS Pro project, and executing the script in various environments. We'll build on the knowledge you gained in this basic exercise in the upcoming

Exercise 3: Using the ArcGIS Pro Python Window

Getting ready

The ArcGIS Pro Python window provides a shell window that can be used to write simple scripts, run tools, or execute Python scripts written with other development environments. It is sectioned into two areas: Python prompt and transcript. The Python prompt is used to enter commands or load and existing Python script. The output from your commands is written to the transcript area above.

How to do it…

Note: Before completing the exercises in this book you will need to download and install the exercise data. Please follow the directions below to download and install the exercise data. You will not be able to complete the exercises in this book until this is done.

Open a web browser and download the dataset from **either**:

Dropbox - https://www.dropbox.com/s/5l5glsmq1gbo7f1/ ProgrammingPro.zip?dl=0

Amazon - http://s3.amazonaws.com/VirtualGISClassroom/ IntroProgrammingArcGISProPython/ProgrammingPro.zip

Using Windows Explorer or File Explorer create a `c:\Student` folder on your computer.

Unzip the downloaded exercise data to the `c:\Student` folder

The final folder structure should be `c:\Student\ProgrammingPro`. There will be a number of subfolders under `ProgrammingPro`.

1. Open ArcGIS Pro and load the `Ex 2A` project found in the `c:\Student\ProgrammingPro\Chapter2` folder.

2. Click the **Analysis** tab.

3. Click the **Python** button.

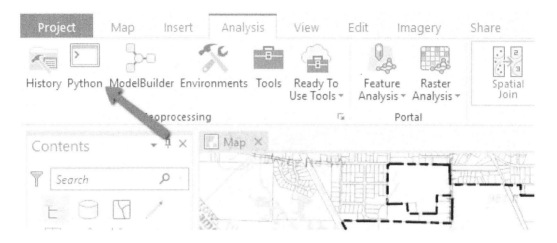

4. The Python Window should now be displayed. The window is divided into two sections: transcript and prompt. The prompt area (small lower portion of the window) is where you write code or load an existing script. The transcript is used to display output from the script.

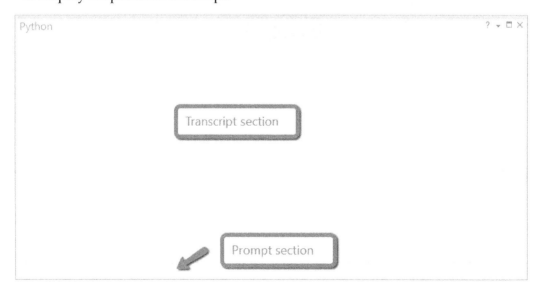

All `arcpy` classes and functions as well as any geoprocessing tools can be called from the prompt. To see how this works we'll enter the `Describe()` function, which is an `arcpy` function that can be used to obtain descriptive information about a GIS dataset.

5. In the prompt section of the Python Window enter the following command: `desc` `= arcpy.Describe()` and pause for just a moment. A list of layers that are in the currently active Map will be displayed as seen in the screenshot below. This is an example of code completion functionality included with the ArcGIS Pro Python window. Select the **Parcel** layer by clicking on it with your mouse.

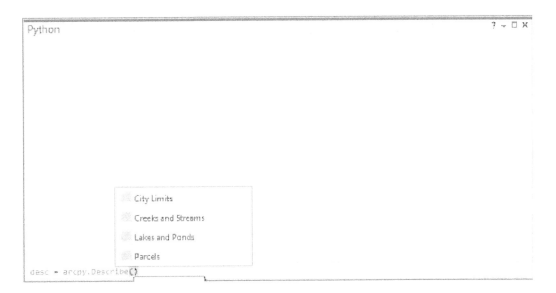

6. At this point the prompt window should contain the code `desc = arcpy.Describe('Parcels')`.

7. Click the **Enter** key on your keyboard. This will create a new variable called `desc`, which is a `Describe` object that contains information about the **Parcels** layer.

8. In the prompt section enter the following code:

```
for field in desc.fields:
    print(field.name + " = " + field.type)
```

9. Place your cursor at the end of the last line, and click **Enter** twice (you have to click **Enter** twice when you are inside a compound statement such as a `for` loop).

This will return the following information to the transcript section if you have written the code correctly.

```
OBJECTID_1 = OID
Shape = Geometry
LOTNUM = String
STNUMBER = String
STNAME = String
STSUFFIX = String
Shape_Length = Double
Shape_Area = Double
Acres = Single
```

10. One of the things that can be a little frustrating about using the ArcGIS Pro Python Window is when you make typos in your code. Since the window executes each command as you enter them, rather than running the entire script as a single entity as in PyCharm, if you make a typo you'll need to retype the line where you made a mistake. Fortunately, the Python Window includes the ability to remember and repeat commands. It keeps track of all the commands you have entered and puts them into a stack of commands with the last command entered being the first to be repeated.

    To see this in action, return to the prompt section, and click the up arrow key on your keyboard. This will repeat the last line of code that you wrote. Click the up arrow key again to see the next most recent command. If you make a mistake somewhere in the code that you type you can simply back up to the offending line of code, make corrections, and re-run that line of code.

11. You can also load existing Python scripts into the prompt section of the ArcGIS Pro Python window. With your mouse, right click inside the prompt section and select Load Code. This will open a dialog that allows you to navigate to the location of a Python script you have saved to your computer. Navigate to the c:\Student\ ProgrammingPro\Scripts folder and select MyFirstScript.py and click Open. This will load the entire script into the prompt section. You can then click the Enter key on your keyboard to execute the entire script at once.

In conclusion...

ArcGIS Pro includes an integrated Python Window that you can use to write geoprocessing scripts using Python and `arcpy`. This window includes code completion and color-coding to assist with the development of your scripts. While not an ideal environment for the development of larger scripts, this window is a good place to begin learning about Python and `arcpy`.

## Chapter 3

Executing Geoprocessing Tools from Scripts

In this we'll cover the following topics:

- Calling ArcGIS Pro geoprocessing tools as method calls
- Passing parameters to the tools
- Overwriting an existing dataset

In this exercise we are going to cover the important topic of executing geoprocessing tools. ArcGIS contains over 800 geoprocessing tools, which can be used in your Python scripts. When executing a geoprocessing tool from the ArcGIS Pro interface you are provided with a dialog box for entering input and output parameters. However, you won't have access to a user interface when running these tools from your scripts. Instead, you call the tools as native methods calls, passing in the input and output as parameters to the method.

Exercise 1: Calling ArcGIS Pro geoprocessing tools from scripts

Getting ready

When you run an ArcGIS Pro geoprocessing tool from a script you don't have the benefit of a visual interface dialog for providing the input and output parameters. Instead, you must call the tools like a method call, passing in the input as parameters. You can also chain together calls to a series of tools, using the output of one tool as the input to another. In this exercise you're going to write a script that buffers the **Lakes and Ponds** layer, creates a selection set of parcels that intersect the buffered layer, and export these parcels out to a new feature class.

How to do it...

1. Open ArcGIS Pro with the `Ex 2A.aprx` file found in the `c:\Student\`

`ProgrammingPro\Chapter2` folder. This project has already been created for you.

2. You should see a map containing several layers including Parcels, Creeks and Streams, Lakes and Ponds, City Limits and a Topographic basemap.

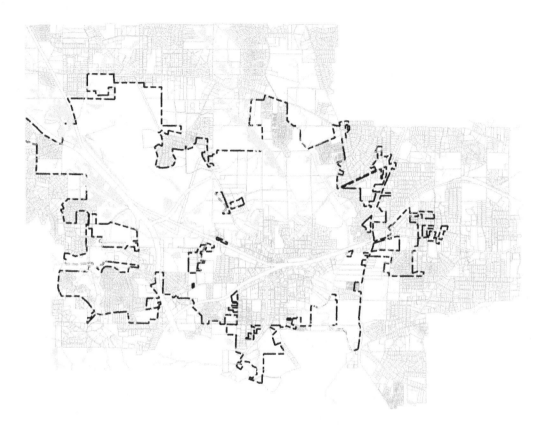

3. Open PyCharm

4. Select File | New | Python File.

5. Name the file `ExecutingTools` and click OK. The file should be written to your default project location of `c:\Student\ProgrammingPro\Scripts`.

6. Import the `arcpy` module and create the basic error handling structure.

7. Import the `env` object from `arcpy` and set the current workspace. The `env` object is used in `arcpy` to set any of the available environment variables. The `workspace` property sets the current working directory for the script. After setting

the current directory, it becomes the default location for any input or output from geoprocessing tools.

```
import arcpy
from arcpy import env
env.workspace = r"C:\Student\ProgrammingPro\Databases\
Trippville_GIS.gdb"
try:

except Exception as e:
    print("Error: " + e.args[0])
```

8. In this next step you're going to use the Buffer tool to buffer the Lakes and Ponds layer. The output from this tool will be used to perform an intersect operation against the Parcels layer to determine which parcels fall within the buffered distance of the Lakes and Ponds.

If you were to run the Buffer tool from the ArcGIS Pro Toolbox you'd be presented with a dialog that prompts you to enter the various parameters. Running the Buffer tool, or any other tool, from a Python script requires that the parameters be passed as arguments to a method call for the Buffer tool.

Add the code below to call the Buffer tool, passing in Lakes and Ponds as the input layer, an output feature layer called Buffered_Water, and a buffer distance of 250 Feet. The output from the Buffer tool will be a feature class called Buffered_Water. We'll use this output parameter as input to another tool in a later step.

```
import arcpy
from arcpy import env
env.workspace = r"C:\Student\ProgrammingPro\Databases\
Trippville_GIS.gdb"
try:

    arcpy.Buffer_analysis("Lakes and Ponds", "Buffered_
    Water", "250 Feet", 'FULL', 'ROUND', 'ALL')

except Exception as e:
    print("Error: " + e.args[0])
```

The output of the Buffer tool is shown in the screenshot below. We haven't run the script yet though so you won't see it right now in ArcGIS Pro.yet.

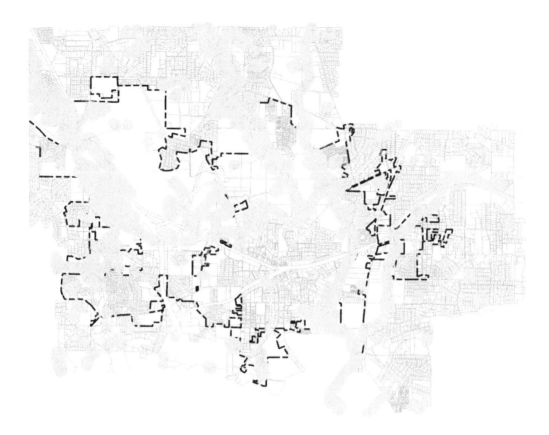

9. The `Make Feature Layer` tool is used to create a feature layer from a feature class. A feature layer is a temporary, in-memory copy of a feature class used specifically for the purposes of creation a selection set with the `Select by Attribute` and `Select Layer by Location` tools. Unless specifically saved, a feature layer will be discarded after use.

Call the `Make Feature Layer` tool passing in the `Parcels` layer to create a new feature layer called `Parcels_FL`.

```
import arcpy
from arcpy import env
env.workspace = r"C:\Student\ProgrammingPro\Databases\
Trippville_GIS.gdb"
try:

    arcpy.Buffer_analysis("Lakes and Ponds", "Buffered_Water",
    "250 Feet", 'FULL', 'ROUND', 'ALL')
```

```
arcpy.MakeFeatureLayer_management("Parcels",
"Parcels_FL")

except Exception as e:
    print("Error: " + e.args[0])
```

10. The `Select Layer by Location` tool will now be used to create a selection set of all parcels that intersect the buffered `Lakes and Ponds` layer. The feature layer created in the last step will be used as input along with the buffered water layer.

Pass the input parcel feature layer created by the `MakeFeatureLayer` tool, a parameter defining the spatial relationship as `intersect`, and the `Buffered_Water` feature class. This will select all parcels that intersect the buffered water feature class.

```
import arcpy
from arcpy import env
env.workspace = r"C:\Student\ProgrammingPro\Databases\
Trippville_GIS.gdb"
try:

    arcpy.Buffer_analysis("Lakes and Ponds", "Buffered_Water",
    "250 Feet", 'FULL', 'ROUND', 'ALL')

    arcpy.MakeFeatureLayer_management("Parcels",
    "Parcels_FL")
    arcpy.SelectLayerByLocation_management("Parcels_FL",
    "intersect","Buffered_Water")

except Exception as e:
    print("Error: " + e.args[0])
```

11. Finally, call the `CopyFeatures` tool with the `Parcels_FL` as the input layer and `Parcels_NearWaterBodies` as the output feature class.

```
import arcpy
from arcpy import env
env.workspace = r"C:\Student\ProgrammingPro\Databases\
Trippville_GIS.gdb"
try:
```

```
arcpy.Buffer_analysis("Lakes and Ponds", "Buffered_Water",
"250 Feet", 'FULL', 'ROUND', 'ALL')

arcpy.MakeFeatureLayer_management("Parcels",
"Parcels_FL")
arcpy.SelectLayerByLocation_management("Parcels_FL",
"intersect","Buffered_Water")
arcpy.CopyFeatures_management("Parcels_FL",
"Parcels_NearWaterBodies")

except Exception as e:
    print("Error: " + e.args[0])
```

The output feature class called `Parcels_NearWaterBodies` is shown in the screenshot below. You won't see this layer until you run the script though.

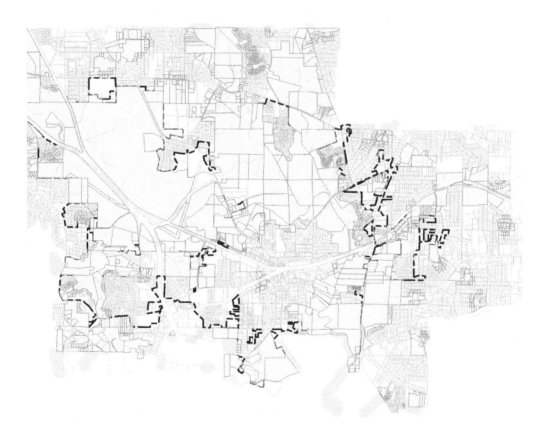

12. You can check your code against a solution file found at c:\Student\ ProgrammingPro\Solutions\Scripts\ExecutingTools.py

13. In ArcGIS Pro with the Ex 2A.aprx project open, load the script you just wrote into the Python window and run it. The output feature class is shown in the screenshot above and you can check the Trippville_GIS geodatabase to see the new feature class as well.

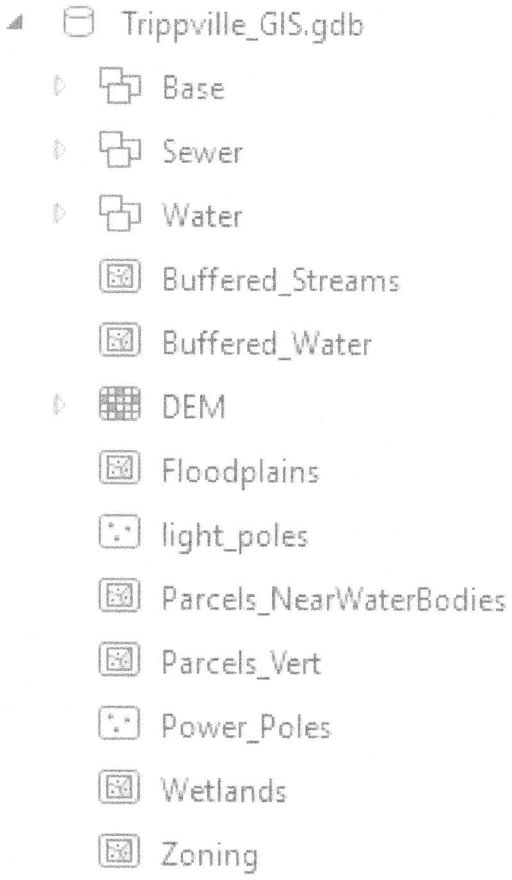

⊿   🗄   Trippville_GIS.gdb

    ▷   🗂   Base

    ▷   🗂   Sewer

    ▷   🗂   Water

      🖾   Buffered_Streams

      🖾   Buffered_Water

    ▷   ▦   DEM

      🖾   Floodplains

      ⦂   light_poles

      🖾   Parcels_NearWaterBodies

      🖾   Parcels_Vert

      ⦂   Power_Poles

      🖾   Wetlands

      🖾   Zoning

14. One last topic we need to cover in this exercise is the idea of overwriting an existing dataset. If you want a script to be able to overwrite an existing dataset you can enable this in one of two ways. You can either set an environment parameter in the script or use the Options dialog in ArcGIS Pro if the script is being run inside the software. To enable the overwriting of an existing dataset you can add the following line of code:

```
import arcpy
from arcpy import env
env.workspace = r"C:\Student\ProgrammingPro\Databases\
Trippville_GIS.gdb"
env.overwriteOutput = True
try:

    arcpy.Buffer_analysis("Lakes and Ponds", "Buffered_Water",
    "250 Feet", 'FULL', 'ROUND', 'ALL')

    arcpy.MakeFeatureLayer_management("Parcels", "Parcels_
    FL")
    arcpy.SelectLayerByLocation_management("Parcels_
    FL","intersect","Buffered_Water")
    arcpy.CopyFeatures_management("Parcels_FL","Parcels_
    NearWaterBodies")

except Exception as e:
    print("Error: " + e.args[0])
```

15. If the script is running directly inside ArcGIS Pro either in the Python window or as a custom script tool (covered in *Chapter 10: Creating Custom ArcGIS Tools*) you can enable overwriting an existing dataset through the ArcGIS Pro interface.

Go to the **Project** tab and then select **Options | Geoprocessing**. There is a check box at the top to allow geoprocessing tools to overwrite existing datasets.

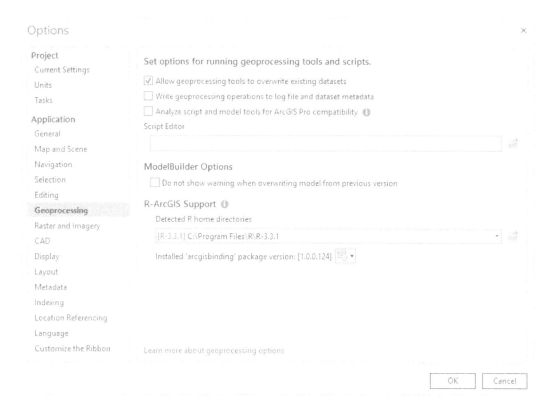

In conclusion...

Any geoprocessing tool found in ArcGIS Pro that you are licensed to use can be called from your script using a native method call. This means that rather than having a visual interface for entering the parameters; you simply pass the parameters as arguments in a method call. This includes any custom script tools that you have access to as well. It is also possible to chain together tools using the output from one tool as input to another tool.

Using Arcpy Mapping to Manage Projects, Maps, Layers and Tables

## Chapter 4

In this we'll cover the following topics:

- Retrieving properties of an ArcGIS Pro Project
- Getting a list of maps and layouts in an ArcGIS Pro Project
- Saving an ArcGIS Pro Project
- Importing a map document file
- Retrieving a map and list of layers
- Adding and removing layers
- Inserting and moving layers
- Working with layer properties
- Applying a definition query
- Setting a minimum and maximum scale threshold
- Applying a `SimpleRenderer` to a layer
- Applying a `GraduatedColorsRenderer` to a layer
- Applying a `UniqueValuesRenderer` to a layer
- Working with Bookmarks

The `arcpy mapping` module brings some really exciting features for mapping automation including the ability to manage projects and layer files as well as the data within these files. Support is also provided for automating the export and printing of maps and layouts, map production and the creation of map books, finding and fixing broken data sources, and more. In this chapter you'll learn how to use the `arcpy mapping` module to manage projects, maps, layers, and tables.

The diagram below provides a visual picture of where the mapping package fits into the hierarchy of the arcpy site package.

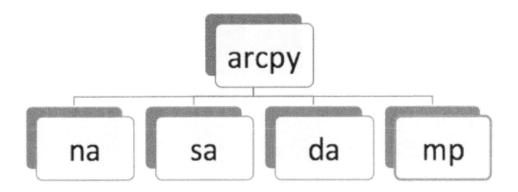

Exercise 1: Retrieving properties of an ArcGIS Pro project

Getting ready

The `ArcGISProject` object represents an ArcGIS Pro project file (.aprx). This serves as the entry point for scripts that use the `arcpy mapping` module. This object can be used to retrieve the default geodatabase and toolbox, home folder, retrieve lists of broken data sources, layouts, and maps, along with additional functions for importing existing map document files and saving the project file.

Before you can actually perform any operations on a project in ArcGIS Pro you need to get a reference to it in your Python script. This is done by calling the `ArcGISProject()` function in the `mapping` module. You can reference either the currently running project or a project at a specific location. We covered this previously in one of the introductory exercises, but we'll cover it again in this set of exercises.

What can you do with an `ArcGISProject` object once it has been retrieved? You can import an existing map document file, generate a list of broken data sources, layouts, and maps, save the project or save a copy of the project, update connection properties, get or set the default geodatabase or toolbox and home folder, or retrieve the last time the project saved, the file path, or the version.

In this exercise you'll learn how to reference an ArcGIS Project, and retrieve properties on this object.

How to do it...

Your first task before attempting any operations on an ArcGIS Pro project is to get a reference to the project you want to work with. This can be done using either the CURRENT keyword or a path passed into the constructor for the ArcGISProject object. After creating a reference to an ArcGISProject object you can then retrieve various properties and call methods.

1. Open PyCharm

2. Select **File | New | Python File**.

3. Name the file ArcGISProjectProperties and click **OK**. The file should be written to your default project location of c:\Student\ProgrammingPro\ Scripts folder.

4. In the new script window import the arcpy mapping module as seen in the code below. This will import the mapping module and store it in a variable called map. Storing it in a variable will cut down on the amount of code you have to write when referring to classes and functions in this module.

   ```
   import arcpy.mp as map
   ```

5. Add the try/except block as seen below.

   ```
   import arcpy.mp as map
   try:

   except Exception as e:
       print("Error: " + e.args[0])
   ```

6. Call the ArcGISProject function and pass in the path to the Ex 2A.aprx file as seen in the code below.

   ```
   import arcpy.mp as map
   try:
       aprx = map.ArcGISProject(r"C:\Student\ProgrammingPro\
       Chapter2\Ex 2A.aprx")

   except Exception as e:
       print("Error: " + e.args[0])
   ```

7. Return the default geodatabase, toolbox, and home folder and then print them out with the lines of code below.

```
import arcpy.mp as map
try:
    aprx = map.ArcGISProject(r"C:\Student\ProgrammingPro\
    Chapter2\Ex 2A.aprx")
    geo = aprx.defaultGeodatabase
    tool = aprx.defaultToolbox
    home = aprx.homeFolder
    print("Default geodatabase: %s \n Default toolbox:
    %s \n Home Folder: %s" % (geo, tool, home))


except Exception as e:
    print("Error: " + e.args[0])
```

8. Return the document version and the last date the project was saved.

```
import arcpy.mp as map
try:
    aprx = map.ArcGISProject(r"C:\Student\ProgrammingPro\
    Chapter2\Ex 2A.aprx")
    geo = aprx.defaultGeodatabase
    tool = aprx.defaultToolbox
    home = aprx.homeFolder
    version = aprx.documentVersion
    dtSaved = aprx.dateSaved
    print("Default geodatabase: %s \n Default toolbox:
    %s \n Home Folder: %s" % (geo, tool, home))
    print("ArcGIS Pro Document version: %s \n Last Date
    Saved: %s" % (version, dtSaved))


except Exception as e:
    print("Error: " + e.args[0])
```

9. You can check your work against a solution file found at c:\Student\
ProgrammingPro\Solutions\Scripts\ ArcGISProjectProperties.py.

10. Run the script. If everything has been written correctly you should see the output
seen below.

```
Default geodatabase: C:\Student\ProgrammingPro\Chapter2\
```

```
IntroArcGISPro Exercise 2A.gdb
Default toolbox: C:\Student\ProgrammingPro\Chapter2\
IntroArcGISPro Exercise 2A.tbx
Home Folder: C:\Student\ProgrammingPro\Chapter2
ArcGIS Pro Document version: 2.0.0
Last Date Saved: 2017-07-21 18:50:52.000505
```

In conclusion...

The `ArcGISProject` object is the focal point of working with the `arcpy mapping` module. It provides an entry point for your scripts and can be used to retrieve properties of a project and to call methods.

Exercise 2: Getting a list of maps and layouts in an ArcGIS Pro project

Getting ready

The `ArcGISProject` object can be used to retrieve a list of maps and layouts in a project.

As you learned in the last exercise, an instance of `ArcGISProject` must be created before calling the properties and methods available on this object. In this exercise you'll learn how to call the list functions for generating a list of maps and layouts that have been created in an ArcGIS Pro Project.

How to do it...

1. In PyCharm select **File | New | Python File**.

2. Name the file `RetrievingArcGISProjectLists` and click **OK**.

3. In the script window import the `arcpy mapping` package.

   ```
   import arcpy.mp as map
   ```

4. Add the `try`/`except` block as seen below.

   ```
   import arcpy.mp as map
   try:

   except Exception as e:
       print("Error: " + e.args[0])
   ```

5. Call the `ArcGISProject` function and pass in the path to the `Ex 2A.aprx` file as seen in the code below.

```
import arcpy.mp as map
try:
    aprx = map.ArcGISProject(r"C:\Student\ProgrammingPro\
    Chapter2\Ex 2A.aprx")

except Exception as e:
    print("Error: " + e.args[0])
```

6. Get a list of `Map` objects in the project and loop over each of them using a `for` loop. Inside the loop, print the name of the map, get a list of all the layers in the map, and print out the names of the layers.

```
import arcpy.mp as map
try:
    aprx = map.ArcGISProject(r"C:\Student\ProgrammingPro\
    Chapter2\Ex 2A.aprx")
    for m in aprx.listMaps():
        print("Map: " + m.name)
        for lyr in m.listLayers():
            print("   " + lyr.name)

except Exception as e:
    print("Error: " + e.args[0])
```

7. There aren't any layouts in this particular project, but the concept is the same. Instead of calling `listMaps()` you'd simply call `listLayouts()`.

8. Run the script. If everything has been written correctly you should see the output seen below. You can check your work against a solution file found at `c:\Student\ProgrammingPro\Solutions\Scripts\RetrievingArcGISProjectLists.py`.

```
Map: Map
   Creeks and Streams
   Lakes and Ponds
   City Limits
   Parcels
   Topographic
```

9. With both the `listMaps()` and `listLayouts()` methods you can also pass a wildcard as a parameter to limit the `Map` or `Layout` objects that are returned. The wildcard is based on the name and is not case sensitive. A combination of asterisks and characters can be used to help limit the resulting list. In the next few steps you'll see how this is done. If necessary, open the `Ex 2A.aprx` file in ArcGIS Pro.

10. In the Project Pane right click Maps and select New Map. This will create a map called Map1. Right click on Map1 in the Project Pane and select rename. Call it Streets and Railroads.

11. In the Project Pane select the arrow next to Databases. Open the IntroArcGISPro Exercise 2A.gdb entry and add the RR_Tracks and Street_Centerlines layers to the map. Your ArcGIS Pro project should appear similar to the screenshot below.

12. Save the project

13. Return to the `RetrievingArcGISProjectLists` script in PyCharm and update your code accordingly.

```
import arcpy.mp as map
try:
    aprx = map.ArcGISProject(r"C:\Student\ProgrammingPro\
    Chapter2\Ex 2A.aprx")
    for m in aprx.listMaps("Streets*"):
        print("Map: " + m.name)
        for lyr in m.listLayers():
            print("   " + lyr.name)

except Exception as e:
    print("Error: " + e.args[0])
```

14. Run the script again. This time you'll notice that the output only contains layers found in the Streets and Railroads map.

```
Map: Streets and Railroads
   Street_Centerlines
   RR_Tracks
   Topographic
```

In conclusion...

A list of maps and layouts can be generated from the ArcGISProject object. You can also use wildcards to limit the list that is returned.

Exercise 3: Saving an ArcGIS Pro project

Getting ready

In addition to having the capability of generating lists of maps and layouts in an ArcGIS Pro project, the ArcGISProject object can also be used save the project or save a copy of the project. The ArcGISProject object includes two methods related to saving a project: save() and saveACopy().

How to do it...

1. In PyCharm select File | New | Python File.

2. Name the file SavingArcGISProProject and click OK.

3. In the script window import the arcpy mapping package.

```
import arcpy.mp as map
```

4. Add the try/except block as seen below.

```
import arcpy.mp as map
try:

except Exception as e:
    print("Error: " + e.args[0])
```

5. Call the ArcGISProject function and pass in the path to the Ex 2A.aprx file as seen in the code below.

```
import arcpy.mp as map
try:
    aprx = map.ArcGISProject(r"C:\Student\ProgrammingPro\
    Chapter2\Ex 2A.aprx")

except Exception as e:
    print("Error: " + e.args[0])
```

6. Call the `ArcGISProject.saveACopy()` method to save a copy of the `.aprx` file and write a message indicating the completion of the script.

```
import arcpy.mp as map
try:
    aprx = map.ArcGISProject(r"c:\Student\ProgrammingPro\
    Chapter2\Ex 2A.aprx")
    aprx.saveACopy(r"c:\Student\ProgrammingPro\
    Chapter2\Ex 2A Copy.aprx")
    print("Finished saving a copy of the file")
except Exception as e:
    print("Error: " + e.args[0])
```

7. Run the script. If everything has been written correctly you should see a message indicating the completion of the script. Open File Explorer in Windows and check the Chapter 2 folder to see the new file that was created.

8. You can check your code against a solution file found at `c:\Student\ ProgrammingPro\Solutions\Scripts\ SavingArcGISProProject.py`.

In conclusion...

You can programmatically save an ArcGIS Project file by calling either the `ArcGISProject. save()` or `ArcGISProject.saveACopy()` method.

Exercise 4: Importing a map document file

Getting ready

ArcGIS Desktop map document files (mxd) can be imported to an ArcGIS Pro project. This method will import the data frames as `Map` objects and the layout to a `Layout` object.

The `ArcGISProject` object includes an `importDocument()` method that provides functionality for convering map document (.mxd), globe (.3dd), and scene (.sxd) files in an ArcGIS Pro project.

How to do it...

1. In PyCharm select File | New | Python File.

2. Name the file `ImportingMapDocumentFile` and click OK.

3. In the script window import the `arcpy mapping` package.

   ```
   import arcpy.mp as map
   ```

4. Add the `try/except` block as seen below.

   ```
   import arcpy.mp as map
   try:


   except Exception as e:
       print("Error: " + e.args[0])
   ```

5. Get a reference to an existing ArcGIS Pro project, call the `importDocument()` method, and save the project.

   ```
   import arcpy.mp as map
   try:
       aprx = map.ArcGISProject(r"c:\Student\ProgrammingPro\
       My Projects\ImportedCrime\ImportedCrime.aprx")
       aprx.importDocument(r"c:\Student\ProgrammingPro\
       Databases\Crime.mxd")
       aprx.save()

   except Exception as e:
       print("Error: " + e.args[0])
   ```

6. You can check your code against a solution file found at `c:\Student\ProgrammingPro\Solutions\Scripts\ ImportingMapDocumentFile.py`.

7. Open ArcGIS Pro and create a new project with the `Blank.aptx` template. Name the project `ImportedCrime` and save it to `c:\Student\ProgrammingPro\My Projects`. This will create an empty project.

8. Close ArcGIS Pro.

9. In PyCharm, run the `ImportingMapDocumentFile.py` script. If everything runs correctly you should see a message in the console window that indicates the script has finished

10. Open the `ImportedCrime.aprx` file in ArcGIS Pro.

11. Open the Project pane and you should see four Maps: Crime, Crime_Inset, Inset_Map, and Test_Performance. There will also be a Layout called Crime. You can see this in the screenshot below.

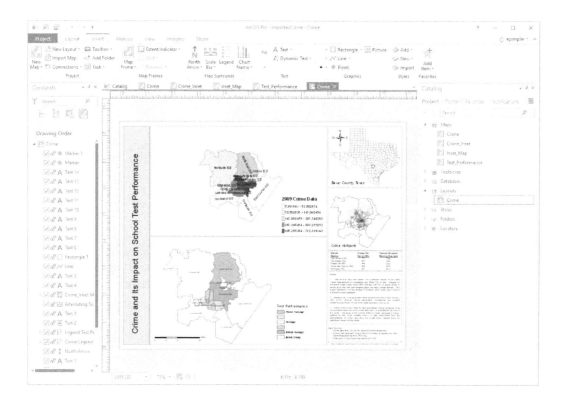

In conclusion...

You can use the `ArcGISProject` object to import an existing map document file created in ArcGIS Desktop. The data frames and layout will be imported along with the data contained within the map document.

Exercise 5: Retrieving a map and list of layers

Getting ready

In an ArcGIS Pro project, a `Map` represents a container for layers and tables, and there can be multiple `Map` objects. Arcpy includes a `Map` object that serves as the primary object for working with these containers. A `Map` object can be accessed through the `ArcGISProject.listMaps()` method or the `MapFrame.map` property.

The `Map` object can be used to add and remove layers and tables, insert layers into specific locations inside the table of contents, move layers to specific positions, clear selection sets, get lists of bookmarks, broken data sources, layers, and tables, and get/set the `Camera`.

A common need in many geoprocessing scripts is to generate a list of layers from a particular map. Often this is just the first step of multiple operations performed by a geoprocessing script. After generating the list of layers it's common to perform some sort of geoprocessing with each of the layers. A `for` loop is typically used to iterate through each of the layers in a map.

How to do it...

1. Open PyCharm

2. Select **File | New | Python File**.

3. Name the file `RetrievingListsMapsLayers` and click **OK**. The file should be written to your default project location of `c:\Student\ProgrammingPro\ Scripts` folder.

4. At this point I'm going to assume that you have enough experience to know how to import the `arcpy mapping` module, reference a project, and create the basic error handling structure so I'm not going to provide explicit instructions on how to do that going forward. Please refer back to previous exercises if you are still unsure how to complete these steps. Go ahead and import the `arcpy mapping` module, add a `try/except` handler, and get a reference to the `Ex 2A.aprx` project located in the `c:\Student\ProgrammingPro\Chapter2` folder.

5. The `Ex 2A` project contains two maps: `Map` and `Streets and Railroads`. Call the `ArcGISProject.listMaps()` method and pass a wildcard to return only the "Map" map (as opposed to the Streets and Railroads) map. This will return

a Python list object containing any `Map` objects that have been called "Map".
Obviously in this case there will only be one.

```
import arcpy.mp as map
try:
    aprx = map.ArcGISProject(r"c:\Student\ProgrammingPro\
    Chapter2\Ex 2A.aprx")
    for m in aprx.listMaps("Map"):


except Exception as e:
    print("Error: " + e.args[0])
```

6. Inside the `for` loop that you just created, add a new for loop that will loop through the list of layers in the map and print out the name of each layer.

```
import arcpy.mp as map
try:
    aprx = map.ArcGISProject(r"c:\Student\ProgrammingPro\
    Chapter2\Ex 2A.aprx")
    for m in aprx.listMaps("Map"):
        for lyr in m.listLayers():
            print(lyr.name)

except Exception as e:
    print("Error: " + e.args[0])
```

7. Run the script and you should see the output below.

```
Creeks and Streams
Lakes and Ponds
City Limits
Parcels
Topographic
```

8. Update the `listLayers()` method as seen below and re-run the script. Here you've introduced a wildcard to the search for layers in a map. It will return any layers that begin with the letter `C`.

```
import arcpy.mp as map
try:
    aprx = map.ArcGISProject(r"c:\Student\ProgrammingPro\
```

```
Chapter2\Ex 2A.aprx")
for m in aprx.listMaps("Map"):
    for lyr in m.listLayers("C*"):
        print(lyr.name)


except Exception as e:
    print("Error: " + e.args[0])
```

9. This script should now return the following:

```
Creeks and Streams
City Limits
```

10. You can check your code against a solution file found at c:\Student\ProgrammingPro\Solutions\Scripts\AddLayers.py.

In conclusion...

The Map object can be used to retrieve a list of layers that have been added to the map. You can also use a wildcard to limit the results that are returned.

Exercise 6: Adding and removing layers

Getting ready

The `Map` object can be used to add and remove layers using a number of methods. You can programmatically add or remove layers using one of several methods on the `Map` object. The `addLayer()` and `removeLayer()` methods provide the ability to add a `Layer` or `LayerFile` to a map in a project. The `addDataFromPath()` method provides the ability to add a `Layer` to a map in a project by providing a local path or URL. The `addBasemap()` method can be used to either add a new basemap or replace one that already exists.

How to do it...

1. Open PyCharm and create a new script called `AddLayers`.

2. In the script, import the `arcpy mapping` module, create a `try/except` handling block, and get a reference to the `CURRENT` map document. You're going to run this script in the ArcGIS Pro Python window.

3. Call the `Map.addDataFromPath()` method and pass in the path to the Floodplains feature class located in the Trippville geodatabase.

   ```
   import arcpy.mp as map
   try:
       aprx = map.ArcGISProject("CURRENT")
       for m in aprx.listMaps("Map"):
           m.addDataFromPath(r"C:\Student\ProgrammingPro\
           Databases\Trippville_GIS.gdb\Floodplains")

   except Exception as e:
       print("Error: " + e.args[0])
   ```

4. Open the `Ex 2A` project in ArcGIS Pro and display the Python window from the **Analysis** tab. In the prompt section, select **Load Code** and navigate to the `AddLayers.py` script.

5. Run the script and you should see the Floodplains layer added to the `Map` object as seen in the screenshot below. A default symbol will be applied to all the features in the Floodplain layer. In a future exercise we'll add some additional code to this script that symbolizes the polygons based on the floodplain type.

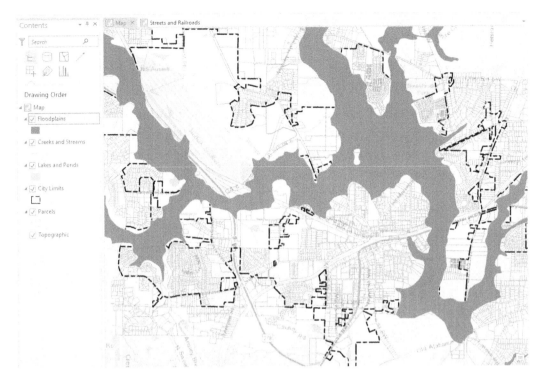

6. You can check your code against a solution file found at `c:\Student\ProgrammingPro\Solutions\Scripts\ AddLayers.py`.

7. What would happen if you altered the `listMaps()` method so that you didn't pass in a parameter indicating which map the layer should be added to?

8. Right now the basemap used with this project is `Topographic`. In this step you'll change this to `Imagery`. In PyCharm comment out the line of code that adds a layer from a path.

9. Call the `addBasemap()` method on the `Map` object and pass in a reference to the `Imagery` basemap.

```
import arcpy.mp as map
try:
    aprx = map.ArcGISProject("CURRENT")
    for m in aprx.listMaps("Map"):
        m.addBasemap("Imagery")
            #m.addDataFromPath(r"C:\Student\ProgrammingPro\
            Databases\Trippville_GIS.gdb\Floodplains")
```

```
except Exception as e:
    print("Error: " + e.args[0])
```

10. Load this script into the ArcGIS Pro Python window and run it to see the `Topographic` basemap replaced with the `Imagery` basemap.

11. While you have ArcGIS Pro open, activate the **Map** tab and select the small arrow just below the **Basemap** button to see a list of available basemaps pulled from ArcGIS Online. You can use the text below any of these basemap when calling the `addBasemap()` method.

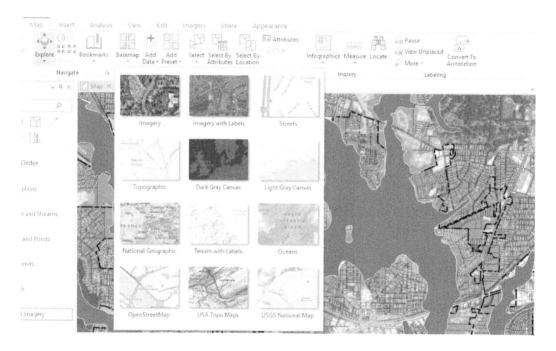

12. The next thing we'll do in this exercise is use the `addLayer()` function to add a `LayerFile` to a Map. In PyCharm comment out the line of code that sets the basemap.

13. Get a reference to the `Zoning` layer file.

```
import arcpy.mp as map
try:
    aprx = map.ArcGISProject("CURRENT")
    for m in aprx.listMaps("Map"):
        lyr = map.LayerFile(r"C:\Student\ProgrammingPro\
        Databases\Zoning.lyrx")
```

```
except Exception as e:
    print("Error: " + e.args[0])
```

14. Call the `Map.addLayer()` method to add the layer file to the map.

```
import arcpy.mp as map
try:
    aprx = map.ArcGISProject("CURRENT")
    for m in aprx.listMaps("Map"):
        lyr = map.LayerFile(r"C:\Student\ProgrammingPro\
        Databases\Zoning.lyrx")
        m.addLayer(lyr)

except Exception as e:
    print("Error: " + e.args[0])
```

15. Add the script to the prompt section in the Python window in ArcGIS Pro and run the script. You should see the output shown in the screenshot below.

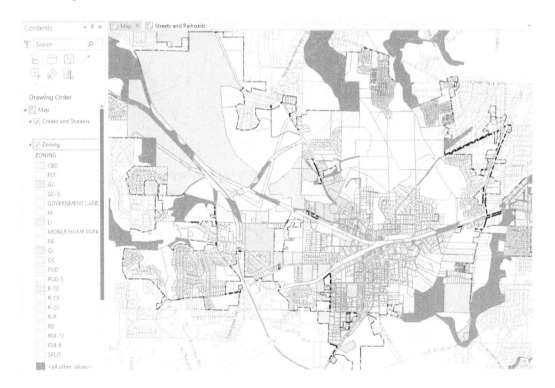

16. Finally, let's use the `Map.removeLayer()` function to remove a layer from a map. Return to PyCharm and comment out the lines of code you added in the last section that added a layer file.

17. Add a `for` loop inside the first `for` loop that gets the `Map` object. This loop should get a list of layers in the map.

```
import arcpy.mp as map
try:
    aprx = map.ArcGISProject("CURRENT")
    for m in aprx.listMaps("Map"):
        for lyr in m.listLayers():

except Exception as e:
    print("Error: " + e.args[0])
```

18. Add an `if` statement that test to see if the layer name is equal to `Zoning` and if so, call the `Map.removeLayer()` method.

```
import arcpy.mp as map
try:
    aprx = map.ArcGISProject("CURRENT")
    for m in aprx.listMaps("Map"):
        for lyr in m.listLayers():
            if lyr.name == "Zoning":
                m.removeLayer(lyr)

except Exception as e:
    print("Error: " + e.args[0])
```

19. Load the script into the Python window and run it to see the `Zoning` layer removed.

In conclusion...

Using the `Map` object in arcpy mapping you can add layers and basemaps using a variety of methods. You can also remove layers using the `removeLayer()` function.

Exercise 7: Inserting and moving layers

Getting ready

For more precise control over where a layer is inserted into the **Contents** pane you can use the `Map.insertLayer()` method. This method uses a reference layer and a position indicator to define whether the layer to be inserted is placed either before or after the reference layer. The `moveLayer()` method works in a similar way, but is used to move an existing layer to a new location relative to the reference layer.

The `insertLayer()` and `moveLayer()` methods on the `Map` object can be used for finer grained control of layer placement. We'll start with the `moveLayer()` method.

How to do it...

1. Open PyCharm and create a new script called `MoveLayers`.

2. In the script, import the `arcpy mapping` module, create a `try/except` handling block, and get a reference to the `CURRENT` map document. You're going to run this script in the ArcGIS Pro Python window.

3. Add a `for` loop that loops through a list of `Maps` called `Map`.

4. Get a list of layers in the map, test each layer to find the `City Limits` and `Wetlands` layers. We're going to use the `City Limits` layer as the reference layer. Using `City Limits` as a reference layer we'll then move the `Wetlands` layer so that it is located just before the `City Limits` layer in the table of contents. `Wetlands` is the target (or move) layer. The target layer is moved so that it is located either before or after the reference layer.

```
import arcpy.mp as map
try:
    aprx = map.ArcGISProject("CURRENT")
    for m in aprx.listMaps("Map"):
        for lyr in m.listLayers():
            if lyr.name == "City Limits":
                refLayer = lyr
            elif lyr.name == "Wetlands":
                moveLayer = lyr
        m.moveLayer(refLayer, moveLayer, "BEFORE")
```

```
except Exception as e:
    print("Error: " + e.args[0])
```

5. You can check your code against a solution file found at `c:\StudentProgrammingPro\Solutions\Scripts\ MoveLayers.py`.

6. Open ArcGIS Pro with the `Ex 2A.aprx` file.

7. In the **Catalog** pane navigate to **Databases | Trippville_GIS.gdb** and add the **Wetlands** feature class to `Map`. Initially it will be added just below `Creeks and Streams`, but our script will move it just above `City Limits` so that it doesn't obscure the `Lakes and Ponds` layer.

8. Open the Python window and add the `MoveLayers.py` script to the prompt section. Run the script and you should see the `Wetlands` layer moved below `Lakes and Ponds`.

9. Now let's take a look at the `insertLayer()` method which works on the concept of reference and source layers. Open PyCharm and create a new script called `InsertLayers`.

10. In the script, import the `arcpy mapping` module, create a `try/except` handling block, and get a reference to the `CURRENT` map document. You're going to run this script in the ArcGIS Pro Python window.

11. Get the `Map` object called `Streets and Railroads`, get a list of all the layers in this `Map` and find the layer called `Street_Centerlines`. Assign this layer to a new variable called `insertLayer`. This is the layer we will be inserting into the `Map`.

12. Call the `Map.addDataFromPath()` method to

```
import arcpy.mp as map
try:
    aprx = map.ArcGISProject("CURRENT")
    for m in aprx.listMaps("Streets and Railroads"):
        for lyr in m.listLayers():
            if lyr.name == 'Street_Centerlines':
                insertLayer = lyr

except Exception as e:
    print("Error: " + e.args[0])
```

13. Create another `for` loop through the "Map" Map object, get a list of layers, and find the layer called `Creeks and Streams`. This will be assigned as the reference layer.

```
import arcpy.mp as map
try:
    aprx = map.ArcGISProject("CURRENT")
    for m in aprx.listMaps("Streets and Railroads"):
        for lyr in m.listLayers():
            if lyr.name == 'Street_Centerlines':
                insertLayer = lyr

    for m in aprx.listMaps("Map"):
        for lyr in m.listLayers():
            if lyr.name == "Creeks and Streams":
                refLayer = lyr

except Exception as e:
    print("Error: " + e.args[0])
```

14. Finally, call the `insertLayer()` method to programmatically insert the `Street_Centerlines` layer at the top of the Map table of contents.

```
import arcpy.mp as map
try:
    aprx = map.ArcGISProject("CURRENT")
    for m in aprx.listMaps("Streets and Railroads"):
        for lyr in m.listLayers():
            if lyr.name == 'Street_Centerlines':
                insertLayer = lyr

    for m in aprx.listMaps("Map"):
        for lyr in m.listLayers():
            if lyr.name == "Creeks and Streams":
                refLayer = lyr

    m.insertLayer(refLayer, insertLayer, "BEFORE")

except Exception as e:
    print("Error: " + e.args[0])
```

15. You can check your code against a solution file found at `c:\Student\ ProgrammingPro\Solutions\Scripts\ InsertLayers.py`.

16. Open ArcGIS Pro with the `Ex 2A.aprx` file.

17. Load the script into the Python window and run it to see the `Street_ Centerlines` layer inserted into the "Map" Map object.

In conclusion...

In this exercise you learned how to use a reference layer to insert and move layers at specific locations within the **Contents** pane of a `Map`.

Exercise 8: Determining layer type and property support

Getting ready

The `Layer` object in `arcpy mapping` represents geographic layers in a `Map` or `Layer` file. This object supports both the older `.lyr` format as well as the new `.lyrx` format. A generic design was used in the creation of this object so that the `Layer` object can represent all layer types. However, not all layers support the same properties. For example, a feature layer supports a definition query, but a raster layer does not.

There are many types of GIS layers that represent different types of data. Rather than creating individual objects to support all the different layer type possibilities, the `arcpy mapping` module uses a single `Layer` object to represent all types. However, the `Layer` object includes many is* properties that can be used for determining layer type. Each of these methods return a `true/false` value depending upon whether the layer is of that type or not. For example, if you call the `isFeatureLayer()` method against a raster layer it would return a value of `false`.

How to do it...

1. Open PyCharm

2. Select **File | New | Python File**.

3. Name the file `LayerTypeAndProperties` and click **OK**. The file should be written to your default project location of `c:\Student\ProgrammingPro\ Scripts` folder.

4. At this point I'm going to assume that you have enough experience to know how to import the `arcpy mapping` module, reference a project, and create the basic error handling structure so I'm not going to provide explicit instructions on how to do that going forward. Please refer back to previous exercises if you are still unsure how to complete these steps. Go ahead and import the `arcpy mapping` module, add a `try/except` handler, and get a reference to the `Ex 2A.aprx` project located in the `c:\Student\ProgrammingPro\Chaper 2` folder.

5. The `Ex 2A` project contains two maps: `Map` and `Streets and Railroads`. Call the `ArcGISProject.listMaps()` method and pass a wildcard to return only the "Map" `Map` (as opposed to the `Streets and Railroads`) map. This will return a Python list object containing any `Map` objects that have been called "Map". Obviously in this case there will only be one. Then, generate a list layers and test each layer to see if it is a feature layer or a web layer. You could include other layer checks for group layers, network analyst layers, and raster layers, but we'll keep this script simple since we're dealing with the more common types of layers.

```
import arcpy.mp as map
try:
    aprx = map.ArcGISProject(r"c:\Student\ProgrammingPro\
    Chapter2\Ex 2A.aprx")
    for m in aprx.listMaps("Map"):
        for lyr in m.listLayers():
            if lyr.isFeatureLayer:
                print(lyr.name + " is a Feature Layer")
            elif lyr.isWebLayer:
                print(lyr.name + " is a Web Layer")

except Exception as e:
    print("Error: " + e.args[0])
```

6. Run this script to see the result seen in the output below.

```
Creeks and Streams is a Feature Layer
Lakes and Ponds is a Feature Layer
City Limits is a Feature Layer
Parcels is a Feature Layer
Topographic is a Web Layer
```

The `supports()` method on the `Layer` object can be used to test a layer for support of a particular property before attempting to apply a property to that layer. This reduces the need for error trapping since you can determine if it's even possible to apply a particular property to a Layer beforehand.

Layers have various properties that can be set. For example, you may want to set a definition query on a feature layer to limit the features that are displayed for that layer. Remember though that not every layer type supports every property so you should use the supports() method first to determine if the layer supports that property. This ensures that an error is not generated when you attempt to apply the property.

7. Update the code in your script as shown below to provide a check to see if the Parcels layer supports definition query.

```python
import arcpy.mp as map
try:
    aprx = map.ArcGISProject(r"c:\Student\ProgrammingPro\
    Chapter2\Ex 2A.aprx")
    for m in aprx.listMaps("Map"):
        for lyr in m.listLayers("Parcels"):
            if lyr.isFeatureLayer:
                if lyr.supports("DEFINITIONQUERY"):
                    print(lyr.name + " supports definition query")

except Exception as e:
    print("Error: " + e.args[0])
```

8. Run the script and the output should indicate the Parcel layer supports the use of a definition query.

In conclusion...

Because the Layer object in arcpy mapping has a generic design meant to support a variety of layers it is necessary to use a variety of checking methods to determine the type of layer and whether a specific property is supported before using it. The is* methods are used to determine the type of layer, and the supports() method queries for the support of a\ specific property before you attempt to use it.

Exercise 9: Applying a definition query

Getting ready

An attribute query can be applied to a feature class in ArcGIS Pro to limit the display of features in the layer to only those that match the query. The Layer object includes a definitionQuery property that can be used to apply the query to a feature layer.

In this exercise we'll build on the code you wrote in the last exercise to set a definition query against the Parcels layer.

How to do it...

1. In the LayerTypeAndProperties script make the following changes. We're going to run this script in the Python window of ArcGIS Pro so that we can see the results so we'll update the reference to the project to CURRENT. Then, use the definitionQuery property to display only parcels where the acres are greater than 5.0.

```
import arcpy.mp as map
try:
    aprx = map.ArcGISProject("CURRENT")
    for m in aprx.listMaps("Map"):
        for lyr in m.listLayers("Parcels"):
            if lyr.isFeatureLayer:
                if lyr.supports("DEFINITIONQUERY"):
                    lyr.definitionQuery = "ACRES > 5.0"

except Exception as e:
    print("Error: " + e.args[0])
```

2. You can check your code against a solution file found at c:\Student\ ProgrammingPro\Solutions\Scripts\LayerTypeAndProperties.py

   Open the Ex 2A project in ArcGIS Pro, load the script into the Python window and run it. The result should be presented as seen in the screenshot below. Notice that only parcels that are greater than 5.0 acres are displayed. You can use an identify operation to verify this by clicking on any of the parcels or you can open the **Properties** window for the **Parcels** layer and go the **Definition Query** setting.

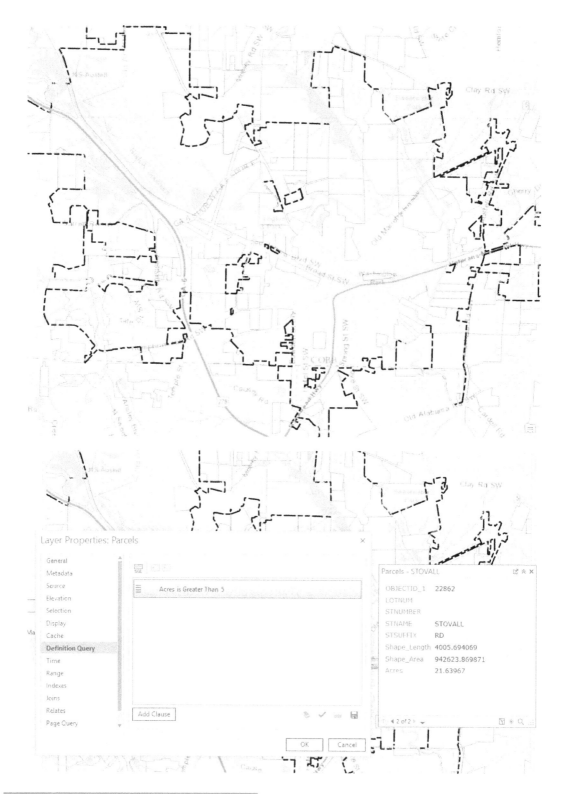

In conclusion...

The `Layer.definitionQuery` property can be used to limit the display of features in a layer to only those that match an attribute query.

Exercise 10: Setting a minimum and maximum scale threshold

Getting ready

Layers that are checked in the Contents pane of ArcGIS Pro are normally visible. However, if you zoom out far enough it may be difficult to see more detailed information associated with the layer. Alternatively, if you zoom in too far, some layers may become too coarse. A visible scale range can be set to help define the scales at which a layer will be visible.

You can programmatically set the minimum and maximum scale threshold using the `Layer.minThreshold` and `Layer.maxThreshold` properties. The minimum threshold is the minimum scale for 2D maps and maximum distance above ground for 3D maps. The layer will not be displayed when zoomed out beyond the minimum scale. The maximum threshold is the maximum scale for 2D maps and the maximum distance above ground for 3D maps. The layer will not display when zoomed in beyond the maximum scale.

How to do it...

1. In ArcGIS Pro clear the definition query that was set in the last exercise. Right click on the Parcels layer in the Contents tab and select Properties. In the Layer Properties dialog select Definition Query and then mouse over the existing query Acres is Greater Than 5 and then click the red X to the right side of the existing query.

2. In PyCharm return to the `LayerTypeAndProperties` script and update it as seen below to comment out the definition query section and add code that tests for the ability to apply a threshold and then apply a minimum threshold so that the parcels won't display out beyond 1:50,000.

```
import arcpy.mp as map
try:
    aprx = map.ArcGISProject("CURRENT")
    for m in aprx.listMaps("Map"):
```

```
        for lyr in m.listLayers("Parcels"):
            if lyr.isFeatureLayer:
                if lyr.supports("MINTHRESHOLD"):
                    lyr.minThreshold = 50000
                #if lyr.supports("DEFINITIONQUERY"):
                    #lyr.definitionQuery = "ACRES > 5.0"

    except Exception as e:
        print("Error: " + e.args[0])
```

3. Load the script into the ArcGIS Pro Python window and run it. After running the script, right click the Parcel layer in the Contents pane and select Properties. Click General and you should see that Out beyond (minimum scale) should now be set to 1:50,000 as seen in the screenshot below.

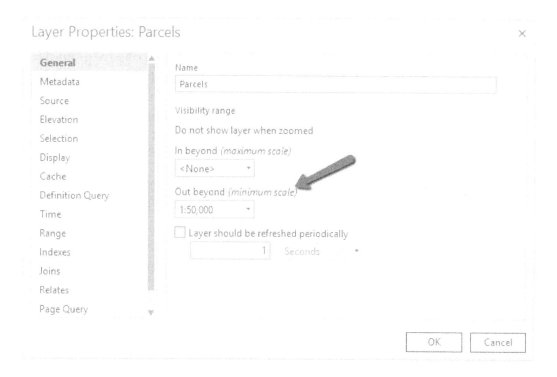

4. In the Map, zoom out until you get past 1:50,000 and at that point you'll see that the Parcel layer is no longer visible. The same process would apply if you wanted to set the maximum threshold so that a layer no longer displays when you zoom in to a specific scale.

5. You can check your code against a solution file found at `c:\Student\ProgrammingPro\Solutions\Scripts\LayerTypeAndProperties.py`

In conclusion...

In this set of exercise you learned some basic techniques for testing layer type, determining if a layer supports a particular property, and applying various properties. In the next set of exercises you'll learn how to symbolize layers.

In this exercise you learned how to use the `minThreshold` and `maxThreshold` properties of a `Layer` object to set a visibility scale range.

Exercise 11: Applying a SimpleRenderer to a layer

Getting ready

The `Layer` object includes a `symbology` property that you can use to return a `Symbology` object. This object can then be used to programmatically alter the symbol rendering of the layer. There is a straight forward workflow for applying symbology to a layer and this includes referencing a layer's existing symbology object, checking to see that the layer supports a specific renderer before making changes, making the changes, and finally applying the changes back to the layer.

The `Symbology` object, returned by the `Layer.symbology` property, contains a single property that gets the renderer and a single method called `updateRenderer()` that is used to change a layer's renderer. The `renderer` property on the `Symbology` object returns the renderer object and can be a `GraduatedColorsRenderer`, `GraduatedSymbolsRenderer`, `SimpleRenderer`, or `UniqueValueRenderer`. In this exercise you'll learn how to work with the simplest type of renderer: `SimpleRenderer`.

How to do it...

1. Open PyCharm

2. Select **File | New | Python File**.

3. Name the file `SimpleRenderer` and click **OK**. The file should be written to your default project location of `c:\Student\ProgrammingPro\Scripts` folder.

4. At this point I'm going to assume that you have enough experience to know how to import the `arcpy mapping` module, reference a project, and create the basic error handling structure so I'm not going to provide explicit instructions on how to do that going forward. Please refer back to previous exercises if you are still unsure how to complete these steps. Go ahead and import the `arcpy mapping` module, add a `try/except` handler, and get a reference to the `CURRENT` project.

5. The `Ex 2A` project contains two maps: `Map` and `Streets and Railroads`. Call the `ArcGISProject.listMaps()` method and pass a wildcard to return only the "Map" `Map` (as opposed to the `Streets and Railroads`) map. This will return a Python list object containing any `Map` objects that have been called "`Map`". Obviously in this case there will only be one. Then get the `Parcels` layer, test to see that it is a feature layer, and retrieve the `Symbology` object.

```
import arcpy.mp as map
try:
    aprx = map.ArcGISProject("CURRENT")
    for m in aprx.listMaps("Map"):
        for lyr in m.listLayers("Parcels"):
            if lyr.isFeatureLayer:
                sym = lyr.symbology

except Exception as e:
    print("Error: " + e.args[0])
```

6. Set the symbol color, outline color, and size on the renderer object, which in this case is a `SimpleRenderer`.

```
import arcpy.mp as map
try:
    aprx = map.ArcGISProject("CURRENT")
    for m in aprx.listMaps("Map"):
        for lyr in m.listLayers("Parcels"):
            if lyr.isFeatureLayer:
                sym = lyr.symbology
                sym.renderer.symbol.color =
                {'RGB': [255, 255, 190, 25]}
                sym.renderer.symbol.outlineColor =
                {'CMYK': [25, 50, 75, 25, 100]}
                sym.renderer.symbol.size = 1.0

except Exception as e:
    print("Error: " + e.args[0])
```

7. Finally, apply the symbology to the layer.

```
import arcpy.mp as map
try:
    aprx = map.ArcGISProject("CURRENT")
    for m in aprx.listMaps("Map"):
        for lyr in m.listLayers("Parcels"):
            if lyr.isFeatureLayer:
                sym = lyr.symbology
                sym.renderer.symbol.color =
                {'RGB': [255, 255, 190, 25]}
                sym.renderer.symbol.outlineColor =
                {'CMYK': [25, 50, 75, 25, 100]}
```

```
sym.renderer.symbol.size = 1.0

lyr.symbology = sym

except Exception as e:
    print("Error: " + e.args[0])
```

8. You can check your code against a solution file found at `c:\Student\ProgrammingPro\Solutions\Scripts\SimpleRenderer.py`

9. Load the script in the ArcGIS Pro Python window and run it. The `Parcels` layer should be redrawn with the symbol style seen in the screenshot below.

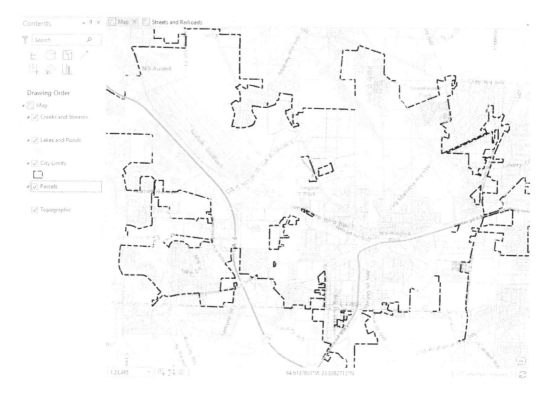

10. You can also use a pre-defined style from the symbol gallery. Symbols have a pre-defined name that can be used in your code. Click the symbol patch for the Parcels layer to display the Symbology pane.

11. Click the Gallery tab and you'll see a number of pre-defined symbols as seen in the screenshot below. Each of the symbols has a name. You can move your mouse

over any of these symbols to see the name. Scroll down until you get to the Extent Transparent symbol. There are several so move your mouse over each of them until you get to the Extent Transparent Wide Gray symbol. This is the symbol from the gallery that we'll apply in the next step.

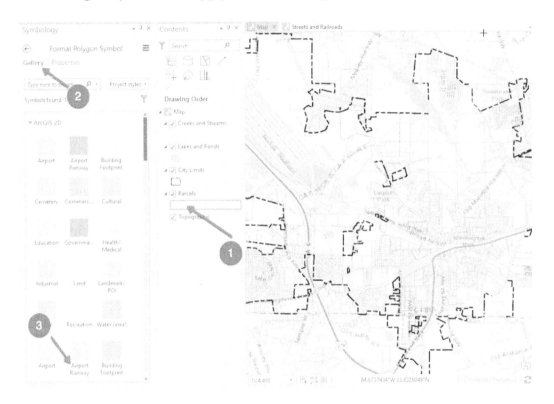

12. Return to the `SimpleRenderer.py` script in PyCharm and update your code as seen below. Load and run the script in the ArcGIS Pro Python window to see how the code updates the symbology of the `Parcels` layer.

```
import arcpy.mp as map
try:
    aprx = map.ArcGISProject("CURRENT")
    for m in aprx.listMaps("Map"):
        for lyr in m.listLayers("Parcels"):
            if lyr.isFeatureLayer:
                sym = lyr.symbology

                sym.renderer.symbol.applySymbolFromGallery
```

```
                    ("Extent Transparent Wide Gray")

                    #sym.renderer.symbol.color =
                    {'RGB': [255, 255, 190,  25]}
                    #sym.renderer.symbol.outlineColor =
                    {'CMYK': [25, 50, 75, 25, 100]}
                    #sym.renderer.symbol.size = 1.0

                    lyr.symbology = sym

            except Exception as e:
                print("Error: " + e.args[0])
```

In conclusion...

The SimpleRenderer object is used to apply a single symbol to all features in a layer. A symbol is typically composed of a color, outline color, and size. This symbol object is applied to a layer to define its display symbology. You can also use pre-defined symbols defined in the **Symbol Gallery** in your code and assign them to a layer.

Exercise 12: Applying a GraduatedColors renderer to a layer

Getting ready

The `GraduatedColorsRenderer` represents qualitative differences in feature values using a range of colors. Feature values for this type of renderer must come from a numeric field. Values are divided into buckets and a unique color in a range is assigned to the individual buckets.

The classification parameters for the `GraduatedColorRenderer` object include `classificationMethod`, `breakCount`, and `classificationField`. The `classificationField` should be a numeric field found on the layer. The classification method (`classificationMethod`) can be one of the following constant values: `DefinedInterval`, `EqualInterval`, `GeometricInterval`, `ManualInterval`, `NaturalBreaks`, `Quantile`, or `StandardDeviation`. The number of classes (or groups) is defined by the `breakCount` property.

How to do it...

1. Open PyCharm

2. Select **File | New | Python File**.

3. Name the file `GraduatedColorsRenderer` and click **OK**. The file should be written to your default project location of `c:\Student\ProgrammingPro\Scripts` folder.

4. At this point I'm going to assume that you have enough experience to know how to import the `arcpy mapping` module, reference a project, and create the basic error handling structure so I'm not going to provide explicit instructions on how to do that going forward. Please refer back to previous exercises if you are still unsure how to complete these steps. Go ahead and import the `arcpy mapping` module, add a `try/except` handler, and get a reference to the `CURRENT` project.

5. Retrieve the symbology for the `Parcels` layer.

```
import arcpy.mp as map
try:
    aprx = map.ArcGISProject("CURRENT")
    for m in aprx.listMaps("Map"):
```

```
        for lyr in m.listLayers("Parcels"):
            if lyr.isFeatureLayer:
                sym = lyr.symbology



    except Exception as e:
        print("Error: " + e.args[0])
```

6. The `Parcels` layer, as it currently exists, is a `SimpleRenderer`. Add a line of code that updates the renderer to be a `GraduatedColorsRenderer`.

```
import arcpy.mp as map
try:
    aprx = map.ArcGISProject("CURRENT")
    for m in aprx.listMaps("Map"):
        for lyr in m.listLayers("Parcels"):
            if lyr.isFeatureLayer:
                sym = lyr.symbology
                sym.updateRenderer
                ('GraduatedColorsRenderer')

    except Exception as e:
        print("Error: " + e.args[0])
```

7. Set the classification field to `Acres` (a numeric field on the Parcels layer), the classification method to `NaturalBreaks`, and the break count to 5 and apply the symbology to the layer.

```
import arcpy.mp as map
try:
    aprx = map.ArcGISProject("CURRENT")
    for m in aprx.listMaps("Map"):
        for lyr in m.listLayers("Parcels"):
            if lyr.isFeatureLayer:
                sym = lyr.symbology
                sym.updateRenderer('GraduatedColorsRenderer')
                sym.renderer.classificationField = "ACRES"
                sym.renderer.classificationMethod = "NaturalBreaks"
                sym.renderer.breakCount = 5
                lyr.symbology = sym
```

```
    except Exception as e:
        print("Error: " + e.args[0])
```

8. You can check your code against a solution file found at `c:\Student\ProgrammingPro\Solutions\Scripts\GraduatedColorsRenderer.py`

9. Load the script in the ArcGIS Pro Python window and execute it to see the result shown in the screenshot below.

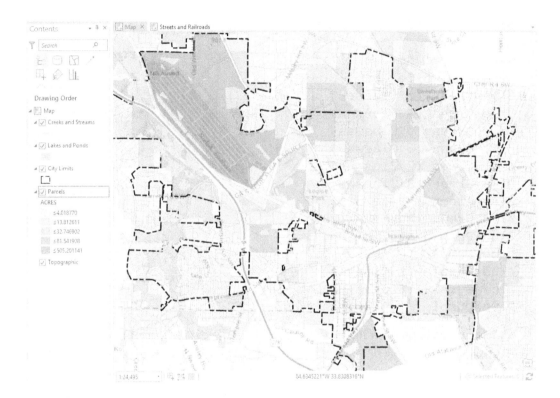

10. You probably noticed that this applied a default color ramp. However, the color ramp can be changed by applying a specific color ramp to the `GraduatedColorsRenderer`. To get a list of the available color ramps, type the following code block into the ArcGIS Pro Python window.

```
aprx = arcpy.mp.ArcGISProject("CURRENT")
for cr in aprx.listColorRamps():
    print(cr.name)
```

11. This will print out a list similar to what you see below. Note, that I'm only displaying a partial list since there are so many.

```
Accent (3 Classes)
Accent (4 Classes)
Accent (5 Classes)
Accent (6 Classes)
Accent (7 Classes)
Accent (8 Classes)
Aspect
Basic Random
Bathymetric Scale
Black to White
Blue-Green (3 Classes)
Blue-Green (4 Classes)
Blue-Green (5 Classes)
Blue-Green (6 Classes)
Blue-Green (7 Classes)
Blue-Green (8 Classes)
Blue-Green (9 Classes)
Blue-Green (Continuous)
Blue-Purple (3 Classes)
Blue-Purple (4 Classes)
Blue-Purple (5 Classes)
Blue-Purple (6 Classes)
Blue-Purple (7 Classes)
```

12. Update your code as seen below. Note: You can select a different color ramp if you'd like. I used Reds (5 Classes) in this case, but you can select something different.

```
import arcpy.mp as map
try:
    aprx = map.ArcGISProject("CURRENT")
    for m in aprx.listMaps("Map"):
        for lyr in m.listLayers("Parcels"):
            if lyr.isFeatureLayer:
                sym = lyr.symbology
                sym.updateRenderer('GraduatedColorsRenderer')
                sym.renderer.classificationField = "ACRES"
                sym.renderer.classificationMethod = "NaturalBreaks"
                sym.renderer.breakCount = 5
```

```
sym.renderer.colorRamp =
aprx.listColorRamps("Reds (5 Classes)")[0]
lyr.symbology = sym

except Exception as e:
    print("Error: " + e.args[0])
```

Load and run the script to see the new color ramp applied as seen in the screenshot below.

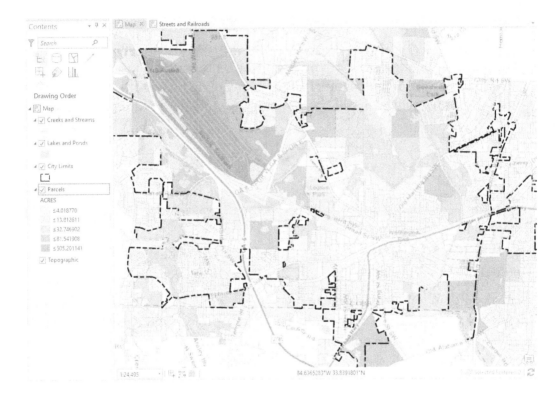

In conclusion...

The GraduatedColorsRenderer object can be used to create a color-coded map based on a numeric attribute field along with the classification method, number of breaks, and color ramp properties.

Exercise 13: Applying a UniqueValuesRenderer

Getting ready

A `UniqueValuesRenderer` applies a symbol to qualitative categories of values. They are used for categorical data including things like flood zones, vegetation zones, planning zones, and soil classifications.

The `UniqueValueRenderer` symbolizes features based on values pulled from one or more fields. It is not limited to just a single field. The `UniqueValueRenderer.fields` property is a Python list that defines one or more fields to use in the creation of the renderer. Immediately after applying the `fields` property, the renderer will automatically generate all the unique values. A default symbol can also be applied using the `defaultSymbol` property. This symbol will be applied to any features that don't fit into the list of unique values.

How to do it...

1. Open PyCharm

2. Select **File | New | Python File**.

3. Name the file `UniqueValueRenderer` and click **OK**. The file should be written to your default project location of `c:\Student\ProgrammingPro\Scripts` folder.

4. At this point I'm going to assume that you have enough experience to know how to import the `arcpy mapping` module, reference a project, and create the basic error handling structure so I'm not going to provide explicit instructions on how to do that going forward. Please refer back to previous exercises if you are still unsure how to complete these steps. Go ahead and import the `arcpy mapping` module, add a `try/except` handler, and get a reference to the `CURRENT` project.

5. Retrieve the `Streets and Railroads` map and the `Street_Centerlines` layer from the map. Test to make sure the `Street_Centerlines` layer is a feature layer.

```
import arcpy.mp as map
try:
    aprx = map.ArcGISProject("CURRENT")
    for m in aprx.listMaps("Streets and Railroads"):
        for lyr in m.listLayers("Street_Centerlines"):
```

```
        if lyr.isFeatureLayer:

    except Exception as e:
        print("Error: " + e.args[0])
```

6. Get the symbology object from the layer, and update the renderer to
   UniqueValueRenderer.

```
import arcpy.mp as map
try:
    aprx = map.ArcGISProject("CURRENT")
    for m in aprx.listMaps("Streets and Railroads"):
        for lyr in m.listLayers("Street_Centerlines"):
            if lyr.isFeatureLayer:
                sym = lyr.symbology
                sym.updateRenderer('UniqueValueRenderer')

    except Exception as e:
        print("Error: " + e.args[0])
```

7. Set the fields property on the UniqueValuesRenderer to the Condition field
   and apply the symbology to the layer.

```
import arcpy.mp as map
try:
    aprx = map.ArcGISProject("CURRENT")
    for m in aprx.listMaps("Streets and Railroads"):
        for lyr in m.listLayers("Street_Centerlines"):
            if lyr.isFeatureLayer:
                sym = lyr.symbology
                sym.updateRenderer('UniqueValueRenderer')
                sym.renderer.fields = ["Condition"]

                lyr.symbology = sym

    except Exception as e:
        print("Error: " + e.args[0])
```

8. You can check your code against a solution file found at c:\Student\
   ProgrammingPro\Solutions\Scripts\UniqueValueRenderer.py

9. Load the code into the ArcGIS Pro Python window and run it. The Street_
   Centerlines layer will be updated as seen in the screenshot below.

10. Just as we saw with the GraduatedColorsRenderer, the UniqueValuesRenderer can be assigned specific color ramps or you can assign the symbols individually for each unique value. The UniqueValuesRenderer object includes a groups property that can be used to retrieve a list of ItemGroup objects. The ItemGroup contains the unique values as Item objects. Add the code highlighted below to see how this works.

```
import arcpy.mp as map
try:
    aprx = map.ArcGISProject("CURRENT")
    for m in aprx.listMaps("Streets and Railroads"):
        for lyr in m.listLayers("Street_Centerlines"):
            if lyr.isFeatureLayer:
                sym = lyr.symbology
                sym.updateRenderer('UniqueValueRenderer')
                sym.renderer.fields = ["Condition"]
                for grp in sym.renderer.groups:
                    for itm in grp.items:
                        print(itm.label)
```

```
        lyr.symbology = sym

    except Exception as e:
        print("Error: " + e.args[0])
```

11. Load this script into the ArcGIS Pro Python window and run it. Now, in addition to symbolizing the layer the script will also print out the values `Fair`, `Good`, and `Poor`. In the next step we'll apply a color to each of the unique values.

12. Add the following code to your script. This will define colors of red for Poor, green for Good, and blue for Fair.

```
import arcpy.mp as map
try:
    aprx = map.ArcGISProject("CURRENT")
    for m in aprx.listMaps("Streets and Railroads"):
        for lyr in m.listLayers("Street_Centerlines"):
            if lyr.isFeatureLayer:
                sym = lyr.symbology
                sym.updateRenderer('UniqueValueRenderer')
                sym.renderer.fields = ["Condition"]
                for grp in sym.renderer.groups:
                    for itm in grp.items:
                        if itm.label == 'Poor':
                            itm.symbol.color =
                            {'RGB': [255, 0, 0, 100]}
                        elif itm.label == 'Fair':
                            itm.symbol.color =
                            {'RGB': [0, 92, 230, 100]}
                        elif itm.label == 'Good':
                            itm.symbol.color =
                            {'RGB': [38, 115, 0, 100]}
                lyr.symbology = sym

    except Exception as e:
        print("Error: " + e.args[0])
```

In conclusion...

The `UniqueValuesRenderer` object is used to assign unique symbols to categorical data from a feature class.

13. Load the script into the ArcGIS Pro Python window and run it to see the result seen in the screenshot below.

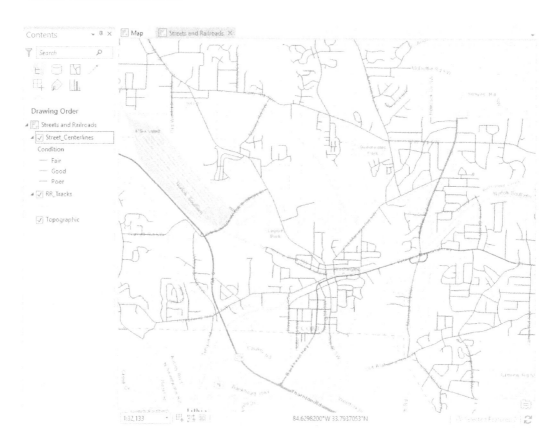

Exercise 14: Working with Bookmarks

Getting ready

Bookmarks are named spatial extents. When the user selects a bookmark from the ArcGIS Pro interface, the map will be redrawn at the spatial extent defined for the bookmark. All bookmarks are associated with and managed by the map. To return a list of bookmarks associated with a map the `listBookmarks()` method on the `Map` object can be called.

Bookmarks can be used for both 2D and 3D views. Thumbnails, which are small images of the spatial extent, can be created and updated using various methods. When a bookmark is created is also sets the `Camera` object properties.

Bookmark functionality is somewhat limited at this point in time. Currently you can get a list of bookmarks, update the thumbnails for bookmarks, and zoom to a bookmark within a `MapFrame`. Hopefully at some point functionality will be added that will allow you to zoom to a bookmark within a `Map` object. In the first part of this exercise you're going to create some new bookmarks using the ArcGIS Pro interface, create a layout that displays a map and some basic information, and then we'll write a script to zoom to each bookmark and export a PDF.

How to do it...

1. Open ArcGIS Pro with the `Ex 2A.aprx` file found in the `c:\Student\ProgrammingPro\Chapter2` folder.

2. On the Map tab find the Bookmarks tool and click the arrow below to display a list of the current bookmarks. There should only be a single bookmark: Washington Park. Click the Washington Park bookmark to see how it works.

3. Zoom to the northwest of Washington Park until you see Legion Park. Zoom in on Legion Park until you are satisfied with the view and then select Bookmarks | New Bookmark. Name it Legion Park as seen in the screenshot below.

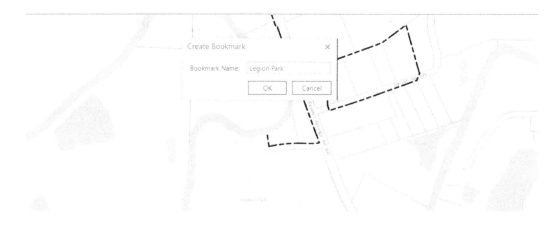

4. Sweetwater Park is due north of Washington Park. Repeat the process of creating a bookmark for Sweetwater Park. You should now have three bookmarks: Washington Park, Legion Park, and Sweetwater Park, as seen in the screenshot below.

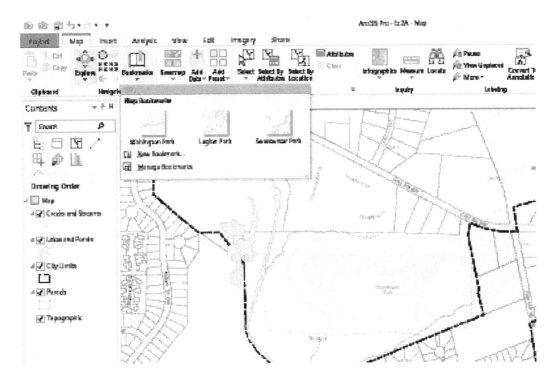

5. In ArcGIS Pro, select the Insert tab and then New Layout | Letter. This will create a new layout in ArcGIS Pro. Rename the layout to Park Layout.

6. With the Layout view active select Map Frame | Default.

7. If you'd like, add some additional layout elements including a title, north arrow, and any other elements you'd like to add. I've kept my layout very simple by adding a generic title and north arrow. In future exercises you'll learn more about how to manipulate the layout and it's elements so we'll keep it simple for now.

8. Save the project in ArcGIS Pro.

9. Open PyCharm

10. Select File | New | Python File.

11. Name the file `Bookmarks` and click **OK**. The file should be written to your default project location of `c:\Student\ProgrammingPro\Scripts` folder.

12. At this point I'm going to assume that you have enough experience to know how to import the `arcpy mapping` module, reference a project, and create the basic error handling structure so I'm not going to provide explicit instructions on how to do that going forward. Please refer back to previous exercises if you are still unsure how to complete these steps. Go ahead and import the `arcpy mapping` module, add a `try/except` handler, and get a reference to the `CURRENT` project since we'll be running the script from the ArcGIS Pro Python window. This will be the `Ex 2A` project.

13. Get a reference to the layout (`Park Layout`) as well as the map frame element (`MAPFRAME_ELEMENT`).

```
import arcpy.mp as map
try:
    aprx = map.ArcGISProject("CURRENT")
    lyt = aprx.listLayouts("Park Layout")[0]
    mf = lyt.listElements("MAPFRAME_ELEMENT")[0]

except Exception as e:
    print("Error: " + e.args[0])
```

14. The next lines of highlighted code will get a list of bookmarks, loop through the list, zoom to each bookmark, and export the layout to a PDF file where the name given to the file is the same as the park name.

```
import arcpy.mp as map
try:
    aprx = map.ArcGISProject("CURRENT")
    lyt = aprx.listLayouts("Park Layout")[0]
    mf = lyt.listElements("MAPFRAME_ELEMENT")[0]

    bkmks = mf.map.listBookmarks()
    for bkmk in bkmks:
        mf.zoomToBookmark(bkmk)
        lyt.exportToPDF(r"C:\Student\ProgrammingPro\
        Scripts" + "\\" + bkmk.name + ".pdf")
except Exception as e:
    print("Error: " + e.args[0])
```

15. You can check your code against a solution file found at `c:\Student\ProgrammingPro\Solutions\Scripts\Bookmarks.py`

16. Load the script in the ArcGIS Pro Python window and run it. The result should be three PDF files written to the `C:\Student\ProgrammingPro\Scripts` folder. You can see an example in the screenshot below. A more complex script would dynamically update the title of the map. You'll learn how to do that in a future exercise.

Park Map

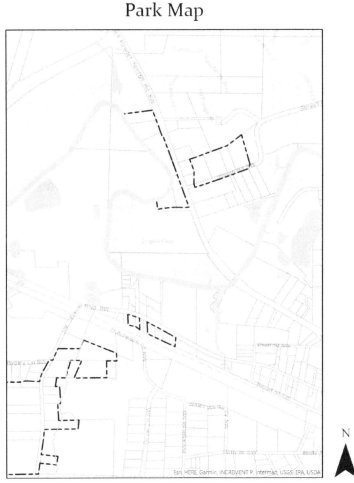

In conclusion...

In this exercise you learned some techniques for working with bookmarks.

Managing Layouts

## Chapter 5

In this we'll cover the following topics:

- Getting a list of layout elements
- Exporting layouts to PDF or image files
- Working with the `MapFrame`
- Manipulating the `Camera`

In ArcGIS Pro a project can contain multiple page layouts. With ArcGIS 10.x you could have only a single layout. Using the `ArcGISProject.listLayouts()` method you can return a list of `Layout` objects which you can then work with through their individual layout element objects. It's important to uniquely name your layout elements in ArcGIS Pro so that they can be accessed individually through your Python scripts. With the `Layout` object you can get and set the page height and weight as well as the page units, export to images or PDFs, and get a list of elements on the Layout.

Exercise 1: Getting a list of layout elements

Getting ready

When a layout is created in ArcGIS Pro there are multiple elements that can be added including maps, legends, text, charts and graphs, map surrounds, and others. Each of these elements can be accessed through unique objects and manipulated in various ways. You can get a list of these individual elements through the `Layout` object.

Each `Layout` that is present in an ArcGIS Pro project can contain multiple elements including maps, graphics, legends, north arrows, scale bars, pictures, text, and others. These elements are represented in `arcpy mapping` by one of a number of objects that represent them. You can use the `Layout.listElements()` method to return these objects in a list.

How to do it...

1. Open ArcGIS Pro with the `Imported Crime.aprx` file found in the `c:\Student\ProgrammingPro\My Projects\ImportedCrime` folder. This project was created in a previous exercise.

2. Open the Crime Layout. You should now see something similar to the screenshot below.

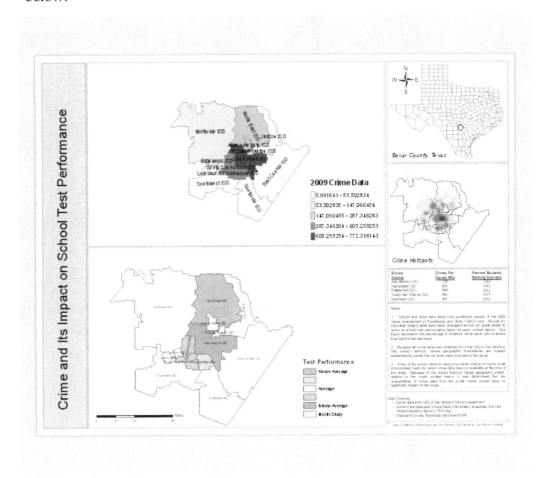

3. An object in `arcpy mapping` represents every element that you add to a Layout. For example the title `Crime and It's Impact on School Test Performance` is represented by a `TextElement` object. Each legend is represented by a `LegendElement` object. You can see an illustration of this in the screenshot below.

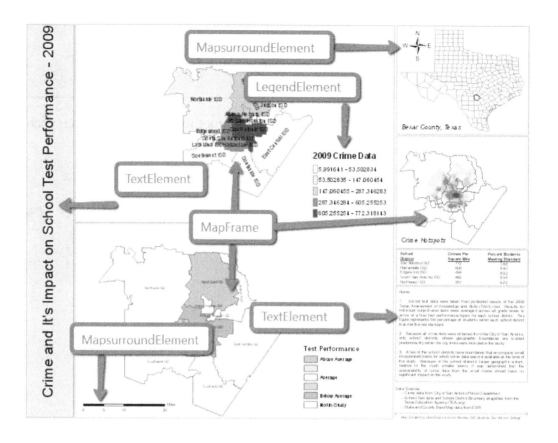

4. You can access any of these individual element objects through your Python scripts via the `Name` property associated with each element. Let's see how this is done. Right click the `Crime and It's Impact on School Test Performance` text item using your mouse and select Properties. This will display the Format Text pane seen below.

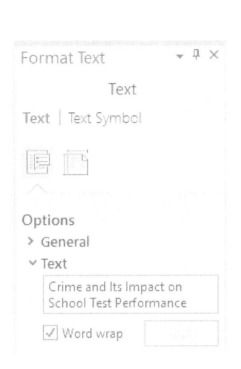

5. Under Options select General to display the Name field seen below.

6. You want to get into the habit of giving meaningful names to each of the elements you add to a Layout. You access the elements by referencing these names in your scripts as you'll soon see. In the Name text box under General Options change the value from Text to Title.

7. Examine some of the other elements that have been added to the Layout and make any changes you'd like to make them more descriptive.

8. Save the project.

9. Open PyCharm

10. Select File | New | Python File.

11. Name the file ListLayoutElements and click OK. The file should be written to your default project location of c:\Student\ProgrammingPro\Scripts folder.

12. Import the `arcpy mapping` module, reference the CURRENT project, and create the basic error handling structure.

13. Call the `listLayouts()` method on the `ArcGISProject` object and pass in the term `Crime` for a specific layout. Get the first item from the list that is returned. This will be a `Layout` object.

```
import arcpy.mp as map
try:
    aprx = map.ArcGISProject("CURRENT")
    lyt = aprx.listLayouts("Crime")[0]
except Exception as e:
    print("Error: " + e.args[0])
```

14. Call the `listElements()` method on the `Layout` object and print out the name of each element. In this first iteration you won't pass any parameters into the `listElements()` method. What this will do is return a list of all elements that have been added to the layout. As you'll see later you can pass parameters to this method to filter the list of element objects that are returned.

```
import arcpy.mp as map
try:
    aprx = map.ArcGISProject("CURRENT")
    lyt = aprx.listLayouts("Crime")[0]
    for el in lyt.listElements():
        print(el.name)
except Exception as e:
    print("Error: " + e.args[0])
```

15. Load the script into the ArcGIS Pro Python window and run it. It should return something similar to what you see below. These represent all the elements that have been added to the Layout.

```
Marker 1
Marker
Text 14
Text 13
Text 12
Text 11
Text 10
Text 9
Text 8
```

```
Text 7
Text 6
Rectangle 1
Line
Text 5
Text 4
Crime_Inset Map Frame
Alternating Scale Bar
Text 3
...
...
```

16. Update your code as seen below and re-run the script to see how this affects the results. Passing in a value of TEXT_ELEMENT as the first parameter will filter the returned list so that only text elements that have been added to the Layout will be returned. You can pass in any type of element based on what you want to return.

```
import arcpy.mp as map
try:
    aprx = map.ArcGISProject("CURRENT")
    lyt = aprx.listLayouts("Crime")[0]
    for el in lyt.listElements("TEXT_ELEMENT"):
        print(el.name)
except Exception as e:
    print("Error: " + e.args[0])
```

17. The second parameter that can be passed to the listElements() method is a wildcard that refers to the Name element. This allows you to further restrict the list that is returned to very specific elements of a certain name. That's why getting into a habit of giving each element a unique name is so important. Update your code as seen below and re-run the script to see the filtered list of what should only be a single object called Title.

```
import arcpy.mp as map
try:
    aprx = map.ArcGISProject("CURRENT")
    lyt = aprx.listLayouts("Crime")[0]
    for el in lyt.listElements("TEXT_ELEMENT", "Title"):
        print(el.name)
except Exception as e:
    print("Error: " + e.args[0])
```

18. Now let's actually do something with that `TextElement` object that is returned. We'll update the title from `Crime and It's Impact on School Test Performance` to `Crime and It's Impact on School Test Performance – 2009`.

19. Update your code as seen below.

```
import arcpy.mp as map
try:
    aprx = map.ArcGISProject("CURRENT")
    lyt = aprx.listLayouts("Crime")[0]
    for el in lyt.listElements("TEXT_ELEMENT", "Title"):
        el.text = "Crime and It\'s Impact on School Test
        Performance - 2009"
except Exception as e:
    print("Error: " + e.args[0])
```

20. You can check your code against a solution file found at `c:\Student\ProgrammingPro\Solutions\Scripts\ListLayoutElements.p`

21. Load and run the script and the title of the Layout should change as seen in the screenshot below.

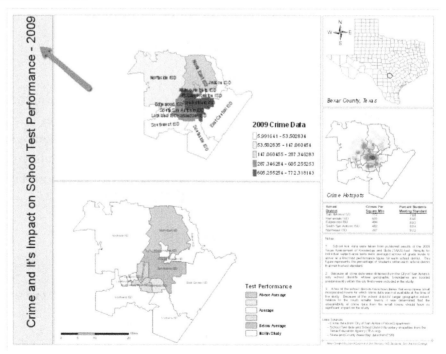

In conclusion…

There are many elements that can be added to a layout in ArcGIS Pro including maps, titles, legends, map surrounds, and others. Each of these elements can be accessed through individual objects found in the `arcpy mapping` module. After getting a reference to an individual element on the layout it is possible to make various changes to the element. They can be resized, repositioned on the layout, and altered in various ways.

Exercise 2: Exporting layouts

Getting ready

Layouts are created for the purpose of creating high quality maps that can be shared with others. This can include printing hard copy maps or exporting the maps as image files for inclusion in a presentation or perhaps the creation of a PDF fie.

The `Layout` object includes a number of export functions that you can use to export the Layout to various file formats including PDF, BMP, EMF, EPS, GIF, JPEG, PNG, SVG, TGA, and TIFF. In this exercise you'll export a Layout to various image file formats.

How to do it…

1. Return to the `ListLayoutElements.py` script in PyCharm and update your code as seen below. The first highlighted line of code defines the output location and file name. The second, calls the `exportToPDF()` method and passes in the output file along with optional parameters for image quality and the embedding of fonts. These define a high quality output resolution and the embedding of Esri fonts so that the end user doesn't need to have Esri software installed to view the map. There are many other optional parameters that you can include for this method. Take some time to examine the help documentation to determine which parameters you should include.

```
import arcpy.mp as map
try:
    aprx = map.ArcGISProject("CURRENT")
    lyt = aprx.listLayouts("Crime")[0]
    for el in lyt.listElements("TEXT_ELEMENT", "Title"):
        el.text = "Crime and It\'s Impact on School Test
        Performance - 2009"
```

```
        outFile = r"C:\Student\ProgrammingPro\My Projects\
        ImportedCrime\Layout.pdf"
        lyt.exportToPDF(outFile, image_quality="BEST",
        embed_fonts=True)
        print("Exported Layout to PDF")
    except Exception as e:
        print("Error: " + e.args[0])
```

2. You can check your code against a solution file found at `c:\Student\ProgrammingPro\Solutions\Scripts\ListLayoutElements.py`

3. Load the script in the ArcGIS Pro Python window and run it. Examine the output PDF file.

4. There are a number of export methods related to exporting various image file formats including `exportToPNG`, `exportToJPEG`, and others. Open the ArcGIS Pro help documentation and examine several of these methods. Pick one and update your script to export the Layout to an image format.

In conclusion...

Creating high quality maps for output to either hard copy maps or image files is a common use of ArcGIS Pro. This process can be automated through `arcpy mapping` and the various export methods on the `Layout` object.

Exercise 3: Working with the MapFrame

Getting ready

When working with a `Layout` it is common to include a `MapFrame`, which is simply a representation of an existing `Map` in an ArcGIS Pro project. There are a number of operations that can be performed with a `MapFrame` including exporting the map to various image file formats, zooming and panning, and others.

The `MapFrame` element, associated with a `Layout`, displays the geographic contents of a `Map`. You can get the associated `Map` object using `MapFrame.map` if you need to make changes to the data referenced by this object. You can also retrieve the `Camera` for a `MapFrame` by using `MapFrame.camera`. Using the `MapFrame` object you can perform a number of operations. You can change the size and positioning of the `MapFrame` on the layout, make it visible or hidden, export to various image formats, get the extent of a layer, pan to an extent, zoom to layers, and zoom to a bookmark. We'll explore some of these operations in more detail during this exercise.

Part 3A – Exporting a MapFrame to image file

How to do it...

1. Open PyCharm

2. Select **File | New | Python File**.

3. Name the file `WorkingWithMapFrame` and click **OK**. The file should be written to your default project location of `c:\Student\ProgrammingPro\Scripts` folder.

4. Import the `arcpy mapping` module, reference the `c:\Student\ProgrammingPro\My Projects\ImportedCrime\ImportedCrime.aprx` project, and create the basic error handling structure.

5. Get a `Layout` object that references the `Crime` layout.

```
import arcpy.mp as map
try:
    # Exercise 3A
    aprx = map.ArcGISProject(r"C:\Student\ProgrammingPro\
    My Projects\ImportedCrime\ImportedCrime.aprx")
    lyt = aprx.listLayouts("Crime")[0]
```

```
    except Exception as e:
        print("Error: " + e.args[0])
```

6. Find the `MapFrame` called `Crime_Inset Map Frame`. It's the one displayed in the screenshot below. You can right click on the inset map and select Properties to display the name of this element.

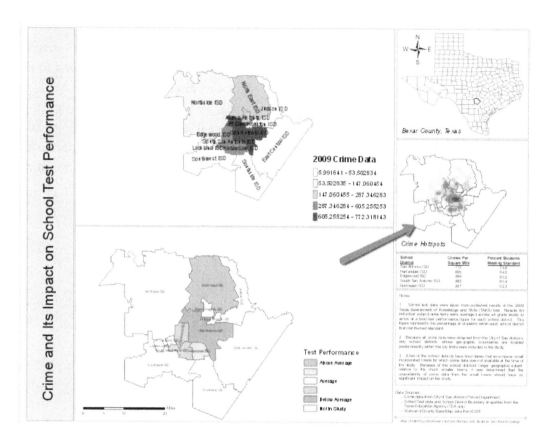

```
import arcpy.mp as map
try:
    # Exercise 3A
    aprx = map.ArcGISProject(r"C:\Student\ProgrammingPro\
    My Projects\ImportedCrime\ImportedCrime.aprx")
    lyt = aprx.listLayouts("Crime")[0]
    mf = lyt.listElements("MAPFRAME_ELEMENT", "Crime_
    Inset Map Frame")[0]
```

```
except Exception as e:
    print("Error: " + e.args[0])
```

7. Define the output file name and call the `MapFrame.exportToPNG()` method to export the `MapFrame` to a file. Examine the output.

```
import arcpy.mp as map
try:
    # Exercise 3A
    aprx = map.ArcGISProject(r"C:\Student\ProgrammingPro\
    My Projects\ImportedCrime\ImportedCrime.aprx")
    lyt = aprx.listLayouts("Crime")[0]
    mf = lyt.listElements("MAPFRAME_ELEMENT", "Crime_Inset
    Map Frame")[0]

    outFile = r"C:\Student\ProgrammingPro\My Projects\
    ImportedCrime\CrimeInset.png"
    mf.exportToPNG(outFile)
    print("Export Inset Map to PNG File")

except Exception as e:
    print("Error: " + e.args[0])
```

8. You can check your code against a solution file found at `c:\Student\ProgrammingPro\Solutions\Scripts\WorkingWithMapFrame.py`

9. Run the script and check the `c:\Student\ProgrammingPro\ImportedCrime` folder to see the `CrimeInset.png` file.

Part 3B – Using the MapFrame to zoom

Getting ready

The `MapFrame` object can be used to zoom to different geographic extents.

In a previous exercise you used the `MapFrame.zoomToBookmark()` method to zoom to an existing bookmark and then export the layout so you are already somewhat familiar with the zoom and pan functions available on the `MapFrame` object. In this exercise you'll learn how to use the `zoomToAllLayers()` method.

How to do it...

1. In a previous exercise on bookmarks you created a new layout called `Park Layout` in the `Ex 2A` project. Open ArcGIS Pro with the `Ex 2A` project to verify that the `Park Layout` exists and if not re-create it.

2. Open PyCharm

3. You can use the `WorkingWithMapFrame.py` script that you used in `Exercise 3A`. Comment out the existing code inside the try block.

4. Reference the current project and get a list of maps. For this exercise we're going to use the `Ex 2A.aprx` file again with the script loaded inside the Python window.

   ```
   import arcpy.mp as map
   try:
       #Exercise 3B
       aprx = map.ArcGISProject("CURRENT")
       m = aprx.listMaps("Map")[0]

   except Exception as e:
       print("Error: " + e.args[0])
   ```

5. Get a reference to the `Parcels` layer.

   ```
   import arcpy.mp as map
   try:
       #Exercise 3B
       aprx = map.ArcGISProject("CURRENT")
       m = aprx.listMaps("Map")[0]
       parcelLyr = m.listLayers("Parcels")[0]
   ```

```
except Exception as e:
    print("Error: " + e.args[0])
```

6. Get the Park Layout and retrieve the only MapFrame object contained within this layout.

```
import arcpy.mp as map
try:
    #Exercise 3B
    aprx = map.ArcGISProject("CURRENT")
    m = aprx.listMaps("Map")[0]
    parcelLyr = m.listLayers("Parcels")[0]

    lyt = aprx.listLayouts("Park Layout")[0]
    mf = lyt.listElements("MAPFRAME_ELEMENT")[0]

except Exception as e:
    print("Error: " + e.args[0])
```

7. The next line of code calls the MapFrame.zoomToAllLayers() method and passes a value of True as the only parameter. This is an optional parameter. If you don't pass in a value of True the method will zoom to the extent of all layers. However, passing in a value of True will zoom to the selected features of selected layers in a map.

```
import arcpy.mp as map
try:
    #Exercise 3B
    aprx = map.ArcGISProject("CURRENT")
    m = aprx.listMaps("Map")[0]
    parcelLyr = m.listLayers("Parcels")[0]

    lyt = aprx.listLayouts("Park Layout")[0]
    mf = lyt.listElements("MAPFRAME_ELEMENT")[0]
    mf.zoomToAllLayers(True)

except Exception as e:
    print("Error: " + e.args[0])
```

8. You can check your code against a solution file found at c:\Student\ ProgrammingPro\Solutions\Scripts\WorkingWithMapFrame.py

9. Open ArcGIS Pro and in the "Map" map, select a handful of features from the Parcel layer as I've done in the screenshot below.

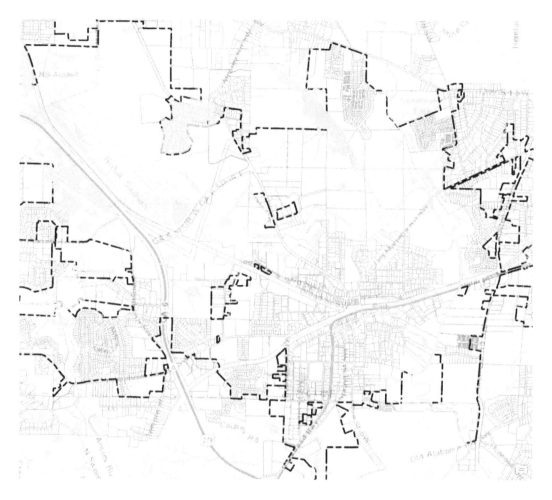

10. Load the WorkingWithMapFrame.py script into ArcGIS Pro Python window and run it.

11. Open the Park Layout and you should see that the MapFrame has been zoomed to the extent of the selected features for the Parcels layer as seen in the screenshot below.

Part 3C – Using the MapFrame to pan

Getting ready

The MapFrame object can also be used to pan the geographic extent. In this brief exercise you'll use the panning functionality of the MapFrame.

How to do it...

1. Open PyCharm.

2. You can use the WorkingWithMapFrame.py script that you used in the two previous exercises.

3. Update your code as seen below. I've highlighted two primary lines that you should focus on. The MapFrame.getLayerExtent() method gets the geographic extent of a layer. The first parameter passed into this method is the layer that the extent will be retrieved from, and the second parameter is a boolean indicating whether the extent should come from the selected features of the layer. In this case, since we passed in a value of True the extent will be the extent of the selected features. The MapFrame.panToExtent() method simply resets the extent of the MapFrame to the Extent object generated by the getLayerExtent() method.

```
import arcpy.mp as map
try:
    #Exercise 3C
    aprx = map.ArcGISProject("CURRENT")
    m = aprx.listMaps("Map")[0]
    parcelLyr = m.listLayers("Parcels")[0]

    lyt = aprx.listLayouts("Park Layout")[0]
    mf = lyt.listElements("MAPFRAME_ELEMENT")[0]

    ext = mf.getLayerExtent(parcelLyr,True)
    mf.panToExtent(ext)

except Exception as e:
    print("Error: " + e.args[0])
```

4. You can check your code against a solution file found at `c:\Student\ProgrammingPro\Solutions\Scripts\WorkingWithMapFrame.py`

5. Load the script in the ArcGIS Pro Python window and run it. The `MapFrame` of the layout should be panned as seen in the screenshot below. Notice that the selected features are in the center of the screen. The `panToExtent()` method doesn't zoom, it just pans so that the selected extent is at the center of the screen.

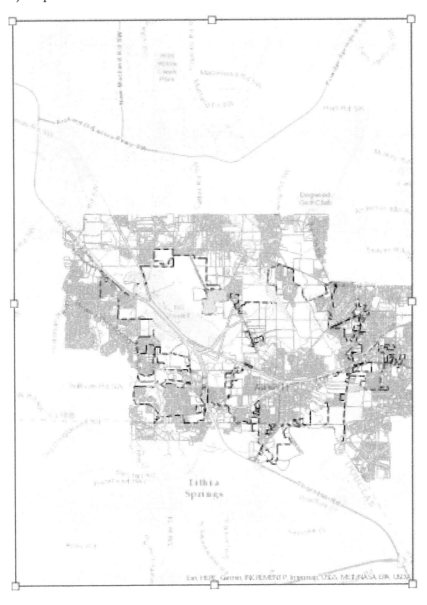

6. Update your script so that it passes in a value of `False` to the `getLayerExtent()` method as seen below and re-run the script to see the difference.

   ```
   ext = mf.getLayerExtent(parcelLyr,False)
   ```

7. Re-run the script to see the difference. The selected parcel features will no longer be at the center of the extent.

In conclusion...

The `MapFrame` object, associated with a `Map` object, can be used to perform various operations including exporting to various image file formats, zooming, panning, and other operations.

Exercise 4: Manipulating the camera

Getting ready

The `Camera` represents both 2D and 3D viewer properties that control the display in a `MapFrame` or `Map`.

The `Camera` object provides access to 2D and 3D viewer properties that control the display in a `MapFrame`. This object can be retrieved using the `MapFrame.camera` property or `Map.defaultCamera` property. Using the `Camera` object you can get and set the extent, change the mode between 2D and 3D or get/set the heading (yaw or azimuth), pitch, roll, scale, and x,y,z properties.

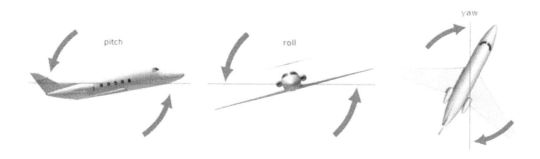

How to do it...

1. You'll need to create a new ArcGIS Pro project for this exercise. Open ArcGIS Pro and create a new project using the `Local_Scene.aptx` template. Save the project with a name of `WorkingWithTheCamera` in the `c:\Student\ProgrammingPro\My Projects` folder. The new project will contain only a single 2D basemap layer called `Topographic`.

2. Right click on the Scene in the Content pane and select Properties.

3. Click the General option in the left-hand side of the window. Rename the scene Union City.

4. Click on the Coordinate Systems option in the left-hand side of the window. Then, click on the Add Coordinate System button and finally the Import Coordinate System option.

5. In the Import Coordinate System window, navigate to `c:\Student\ProgrammingPro\Databases\UnionCity.gdb`. Select the DEM raster and click on the OK button. This sets your scene, so it will use the same coordinate system as the DEM and other layers you will add to the scene during the exercise.

6. Click OK in the Map Properties window.

7. In the Catalog pane, right click on Databases and select Add Database. Navigate to `c:\Student\ProgrammingPro\Databases` and select `UnionCity.gdb`. Click the OK button to add this existing geodatabase to the project.

8. Right click on the Union City scene in the Content pane and select Properties.

9. Click Elevation Surface from the left hand side of the window.

10. Click Elevation sources and then Add Elevation Source.

11. Select DEM from the UnionCity geodatabase.

12. Remove the default Terrain3D elevation source by clicking on the red X button.

13. Click the Map tab and the Add Data button.

14. Navigate to the `c:\Student\ProgrammingPro\Chapter5` folder and select 3D Buildings.lyrx.

15. The buildings will initially appear very small so zoom in on the view until it looks similar to what you see in the screenshot below. It doesn't have to be exact though.

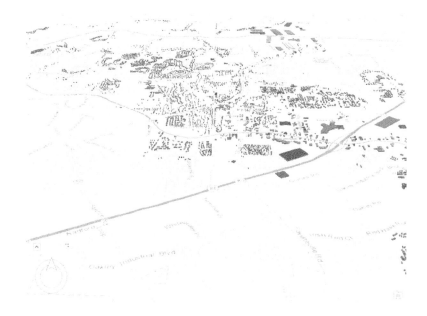

16. In ArcGIS Pro select the Insert tab and then New Layout | Landscape Letter.

17. Rename the newly created layout to Union City Layout.

18. On the Insert tab select MapFrame | Union City to add a new MapFrame to the view as seen in the screenshot below.

19. Open PyCharm

20. Select File | New | Python File.

21. Name the file `WorkingWithCamera` and click OK. The file should be written to your default project location of `c:\Student\ProgrammingPro\Scripts` folder.

22. Import the `arcpy mapping` module, reference the `CURRENT` project, and create the basic error handling structure.

23. Initially we're just going to retrieve the 3D properties of the `Camera` object and then later we'll set some of the properties to see the affect. Retrieve the `Union City` map, the `Union City Layout`, and the `MAPFRAME_ELEMENT` with the code below.

```
import arcpy.mp as map
try:
    aprx = map.ArcGISProject("CURRENT")
    m = aprx.listMaps("Union City")[0]
    lyt = aprx.listLayouts("Union City Layout")[0]
    mf = lyt.listElements("MAPFRAME_ELEMENT")[0]

except Exception as e:
    print("Error: " + e.args[0])
```

24. Retrieve the `Camera` object from the `MapFrame`.

```
import arcpy.mp as map
try:
    aprx = map.ArcGISProject("CURRENT")
    m = aprx.listMaps("Union City")[0]

    lyt = aprx.listLayouts("Union City Layout")[0]
    mf = lyt.listElements("MAPFRAME_ELEMENT")[0]
    camera = mf.camera

except Exception as e:
    print("Error: " + e.args[0])
```

25. Check to see that the map is in 3D and if so, get the camera `pitch`, `heading`, `roll`, `X`, `Y`, and `Z` properties and print them out.

```
import arcpy.mp as map
try:
```

```
aprx = map.ArcGISProject("CURRENT")
m = aprx.listMaps("Union City")[0]

lyt = aprx.listLayouts("Union City Layout")[0]
mf = lyt.listElements("MAPFRAME_ELEMENT")[0]
camera = mf.camera

if camera.mode == "LOCAL":   #check to make sure it's 3D
    print("Pitch: " + str(camera.pitch))
    print("Heading: " + str(camera.heading))
    print("Roll: " + str(camera.roll))
    print("X: " + str(camera.X))
    print("Y: " + str(camera.Y))
    print("Z: " + str(camera.Z))

except Exception as e:
    print("Error: " + e.args[0])
```

26. You can check your code against a solution file found at `c:\Student\ProgrammingPro\Solutions\Scripts\WorkingWithCamera.py`

27. In ArcGIS Pro make Union City Layout the active view.

28. Load the script in the ArcGIS Pro Python window and run it. The results should appear similar to what you see below. Keep in mind though that your results will probably differ somewhat from mine due to slight differences in how you initially set the display.

```
Pitch: -20.0
Heading: 0.0
Roll: 0.0
X: 2174926.9290598724
Y: 1298845.05538592
Z: 3445.140564667932
```

29. Now we'll change some of the properties to see how it affects the display.

30. Return to the `WorkingWithCamera` script in PyCharm.

31. The `pitch` property is the equivalent of moving a plane's nose up or down with the axis passing directly through the wings of the plane. Values can range from -90 to +90. Positive values are above the horizon and negative values are below the horizon. For example, a value of -90 would be looking down on the map, while a

value of +90 would be looking directly up. Alter your code as seen below and run the script in ArcGIS Pro. You screenshot may differ from what you see below, but the view should be pointing directly down (-90).

```
import arcpy.mp as map
try:
    aprx = map.ArcGISProject("CURRENT")
    m = aprx.listMaps("Union City")[0]

    lyt = aprx.listLayouts("Union City Layout")[0]
    mf = lyt.listElements("MAPFRAME_ELEMENT")[0]
    camera = mf.camera

    if camera.mode == "LOCAL":   #check to make sure it's 3D
        camera.pitch = -90.00

except Exception as e:
    print("Error: " + e.args[0])
```

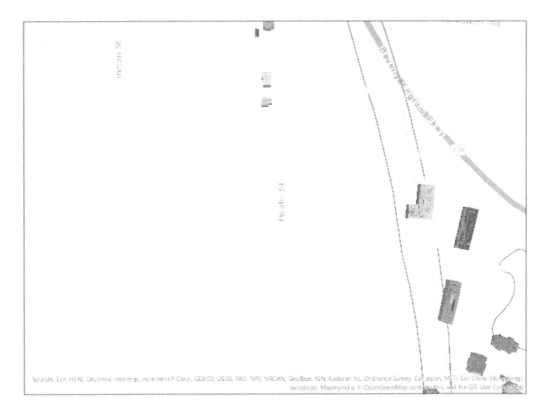

32. In the ArcGIS Pro Python window, put the cursor inside the Python prompt and click the up arrow key on your keyboard to display the code you last executed. Change the `pitch` property to some other value such as -45 and run it again to see the affect. Run this script a number of times with different values to get a good feel for how the pitch property works. Values can range from -90 to +90 with 0 being toward the horizon.

33. The `roll` property is the equivalent of tilting a plane's wings up or down. A zero value is perfectly horizontal. Positive values will tilt the right side upward. Negative values do the opposite.

```
import arcpy.mp as map
try:
    aprx = map.ArcGISProject("CURRENT")
    m = aprx.listMaps("Union City")[0]

    lyt = aprx.listLayouts("Union City Layout")[0]
    mf = lyt.listElements("MAPFRAME_ELEMENT")[0]
    camera = mf.camera

    if camera.mode == "LOCAL":   #check to make sure it's 3D
        camera.pitch = 0.00
        camera.roll = 45

except Exception as e:
    print("Error: " + e.args[0])
```

34. You should now see something similar to the screenshot below, but note that your view may be somewhat different.

35. The `heading` property provides the ability to either get or set the map view rotation value. This is also known as yaw or azimuth. It represents the number of degrees by which the map's data will be rotated, measured counter-clockwise from the north. You can use negative values to rotate clockwise. Update the script as seen below and run it in ArcGIS Pro to see the effect.

```
import arcpy.mp as map
try:
    aprx = map.ArcGISProject("CURRENT")
    m = aprx.listMaps("Union City")[0]

    lyt = aprx.listLayouts("Union City Layout")[0]
    mf = lyt.listElements("MAPFRAME_ELEMENT")[0]
    camera = mf.camera

    if camera.mode == "LOCAL":   #check to make sure it's 3D
        camera.pitch = 0.00
        camera.roll = 0.00
        camera.heading = 90.00
```

```
except Exception as e:
    print("Error: " + e.args[0]
```

In conclusion...

In this exercise you learned how to use the `Camera` object associated with a `MapFrame` object to control the display characteristics of a 3D scene.

## Chapter 6

Automating Map Production

In this chapter we'll cover the following topics:

- Enabling a map series in an ArcGIS Pro layout
- Automating the production of a map series with `arcpy mapping`

Many organizations have a need to create a series of individual maps that cover a larger geographical area. Previously called map books in ArcGIS Desktop, but now known as a map series in ArcGIS Pro, these documents contain a series of maps and some optional additional pages including title pages, an overview map, and some other ancillary information such as charts, reports, and tables. This information is joined together into a single document in the form of a PDF file. While the terminology has changed with ArcGIS Pro, much of the workflow for automating the creation of a map series is similar.

For example, a utility company might want to generate a map series detailing their assets across a service area. A map series for this utility company could include a series of maps, each at a large scale, along with a title page and an overview map. These resources would then be joined together into a single document that could be printed or distributed as a PDF file.

A map series uses a single layout document from an ArcGIS Pro project. The layout contains data including operational data and a basemap along with an index layer. The index layer is used to define the geographic extent of each page in the map series. Each page contains data for the extent of that map in the series. The layout typically includes other information such as a title, descriptive text, north arrows, scale bars, and other elements.

The `arcpy mapping` module can be used to automate the process of creating the output PDF file that contains the map series. Through the `PDFDocument` class in the `mapping` module you can create new PDF files, attach documents, set document security settings, and more.

Exercise 1: Enabling a map series in an ArcGIS Pro layout

Getting ready

To create a map series in an ArcGIS Pro project you must first enable this functionality for a layout. Enabling map series functionality is done through an active layout view by clicking **Map Series** under **Page Layout**. This will display a properties dialog that requires several parameters. In the exercise below you will learn how to enable a map series for a layout. In this exercise you are going to enable a map series on a layout that will ultimately allow you to write a script that automates the creation of a map series that displays topographic data for King County, WA.

How to do it...

It's beyond the scope of this book to cover all the details of creating a map series. Instead, we are going to focus on the aspects of a map series that can be automated through the use of a Python script that uses the `arcpy mapping` module. To save time we have done some of the work for you including the creation of an index grid layer. In this exercise you will focus on enabling map series functionality in an ArcGIS Pro project, and automating the process of creating each map in the series through an `arcpy` script in the next exercise.

1. Open ArcGIS Pro and load the `MapSeries.aprx` project found in `c:\Student\ProgrammingPro\Chapter6\MapSeries`. As I mentioned earlier some of the work for this project has already been done for you. In addition to creating the index grid layer we have already created a detail map, locator map, and a layout with two `MapFrames`, a north arrow, scale bar, and some text. This will allow you to focus on the aspects of the project that deal with automating the creation of the map series.

2. In the Catalog view open the Layouts folder and you should see a single layout called Topographic. Double click the Topographic layout to display the view as seen in the screenshot below.

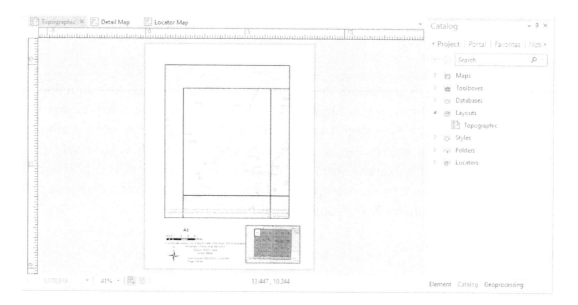

3. In the Catalog view open the Maps folder and you should see two maps: Detail Map and Locator Map. The Locator Map, seen in the screenshot below, is used as the MapFrame for the overview map on the layout. The detail map includes the grid index features and the basemap. If you had operational data to go along with the basemap it would be included on the Detail Map as well, but we're keeping things simple in this exercise so you can focus on automation.

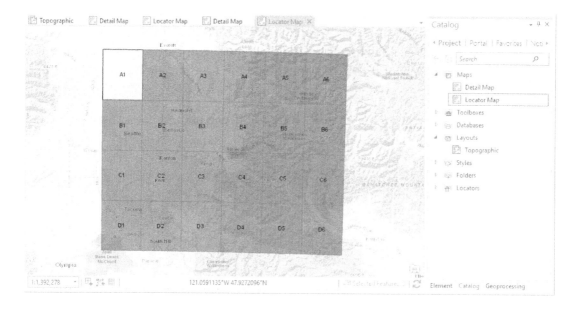

4. Activate the Topographic layout and then select the Layout tab.

5. Click the drop down arrow for Map Series in the Page Setup section and select Spatial to display the Layout Properties dialog seen in the screenshot below.

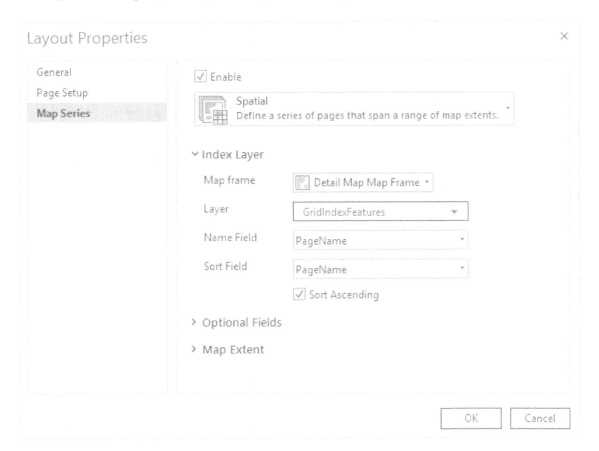

6. First we'll set the properties that define the Index Layer. Set the following properties:
   - Map frame: Detail Map Map Frame
   - Layer: GridIndexFeatures
   - Name Field: PageName
   - Sort Field: PageNumber
   - Sort Ascending: Checked

7. Under Index Layer | Map Frame you have two options: Detail Map Map Frame or Locator Map Map Frame. Select Detail Map Map Frame.

8. Leave the default properties under Optional Fields.

9. Under Map Extent select Best Fit Extent with a Margin Size of 25 Percent and Round scale to nearest 10.

10. Click OK. This will enable map series functionality for the project.

11. Save the project.

In conclusion...

The creation of a map series includes several components including an index layer, basemap, operational data, a layout that includes the data and layout elements, and the configuration of map series parameters. In this exercise you learned how to enable a map series for a layout by setting various properties including the index layer, map extent, and optional fields. In the next exercise you will learn how to create a Python script that uses `arcpy mapping` module along with a map series to automate the process of creating a PDF file that contains the map series.

Exercise 2: Automating the production of a map series using arcpy mapping

> As of the time this chapter was written (ArcGIS Pro 2.0), Esri has not yet released the `MapSeries` object, which will greatly simplify the task of automating the creation of a map series using Python and `arcpy`. Esri is planning to release this functionality at version 2.1 or 2.2. Until then I have designed this exercise as a general-purpose workaround for the lack of this object. When working with ArcGIS Desktop and the `arcpy.mapping` module, the `DataDrivenPages` object was used to automate the creation of map books. The new `MapSeries` object, when it is released, will replicate this functionality and provide some additional functions beyond the old `DataDrivenPages` object. This exercise will be updated when this object is available.

Getting ready

In addition to exporting your maps to PDF you can also manipulate existing PDF documents or create new PDF documents. You can merge pages, set document open behavior, add file attachments, and create or change document security settings. The `PDFDocumentOpen()` function is used to open an existing PDF file for manipulation. `PDFDocumentCreate()` creates a new PDF document. These functions are often used in the creation of a map series, as you'll see in this exercise.

You'll need to use `PDFDocumentCreate` to create a new PDF document by providing a path and filename for the document. The PDF is not actually created on disk until you insert or append pages and then call `PDFDocument.saveAndClose()`. The `appendPages()` and `insertPages()` functions are used to insert and append pages.

`PDFDocumentOpen` accepts a parameter that specifies the path to a PDF file and returns an instance of `PDFDocument`. Once open you can make modifications to PDF file properties, add or insert files, and attach documents. Make sure you call `PDFDocument.saveAndClose()` after all operations to save the changes to disk.

In this exercise you will use the `PDFDocument` object and `arcpy mapping` module to automate the creation of a map series as a PDF document.

How to do it...

1. Open PyCharm

2. Select **File | New | Python File**.

3. Name the file `CreateMapSeries` and click **OK**. The file should be written to your default project location of `c:\Student\ProgrammingPro\Scripts` folder.

4. Import the `arcpy` and `os` modules, set up a basic `try/except` structure, and get a reference to the `MapSeries.aprx` project found at `c:\Student\ProgrammingPro\Chapter6\MapSeries` folder.

5. Set the workspace.

```
import arcpy
import os

try:
    aprx = arcpy.mp.ArcGISProject(r"c:\Student\
    ProgrammingPro\Chapter6\MapSeries\MapSeries.aprx")
    arcpy.env.workspace = r"C:\Student\ProgrammingPro\
    Databases\MapBook.gdb"

except Exception as e:
    print("Error: " + e.args[0])
```

6. Create an output directory variable.

```
import arcpy
import os

try:
    aprx = arcpy.mp.ArcGISProject(r"c:\Student\
    ProgrammingPro\Chapter6\MapSeries\MapSeries.aprx")
    arcpy.env.workspace = r"C:\Student\ProgrammingPro\
    Databases\MapBook.gdb"
    outDir = r"C:\Student\ProgrammingPro\Chapter6"

except Exception as e:
     print("Error: " + e.args[0])
```

7. Create a new, empty PDF document in the specified output directory. This block of code will also use the Python `os` module to delete this file if it already exists.

```
import arcpy
import os

try:
    aprx = arcpy.mp.ArcGISProject(r"c:\Student\
    ProgrammingPro\Chapter6\MapSeries\MapSeries.aprx")
    arcpy.env.workspace = r"C:\Student\ProgrammingPro\
    Databases\MapBook.gdb"

    outDir = r"C:\Student\ProgrammingPro\Chapter6"
    finalpdf_filename = outDir + r"\MapSeries.pdf"
    if os.path.exists(finalpdf_filename):
        os.remove(finalpdf_filename)
    finalPdf = arcpy.mp.PDFDocumentCreate(finalpdf_filename)

except Exception as e:
    print("Error: " + e.args[0])
```

8. Add the title page to the PDF.

```
import arcpy
import os

try:
    aprx = arcpy.mp.ArcGISProject(r"c:\Student\
    ProgrammingPro\Chapter6\MapSeries\MapSeries.aprx")
    arcpy.env.workspace = r"C:\Student\ProgrammingPro\
    Databases\MapBook.gdb"

    outDir = r"C:\Student\ProgrammingPro\Chapter6"
    finalpdf_filename = outDir + r"\MapSeries.pdf"
    if os.path.exists(finalpdf_filename):
        os.remove(finalpdf_filename)
    finalPdf = arcpy.mp.PDFDocumentCreate(finalpdf_filename)

    # Add the title page to the pdf
    print("Adding the title page  \n")
    finalPdf.appendPages(outDir + r"\TitlePage.pdf")

except Exception as e:
    print("Error: " + e.args[0])
```

9. Add the index map to the PDF.

```
import arcpy
import os

try:
    aprx = arcpy.mp.ArcGISProject(r"c:\Student\
    ProgrammingPro\Chapter6\MapSeries\MapSeries.aprx")
    arcpy.env.workspace = r"C:\Student\ProgrammingPro\
    Databases\MapBook.gdb"

    outDir = r"C:\Student\ProgrammingPro\Chapter6"
    finalpdf_filename = outDir + r"\MapSeries.pdf"
    if os.path.exists(finalpdf_filename):
        os.remove(finalpdf_filename)
    finalPdf = arcpy.mp.PDFDocumentCreate(finalpdf_filename)

    # Add the title page to the pdf
    print("Adding the title page  \n")
    finalPdf.appendPages(outDir + r"\TitlePage.pdf")

    #Add the index map to the pdf
    print("Adding the index page  \n")
    finalPdf.appendPages(outDir + r"\MapIndex.pdf")

except Exception as e:
    print("Error: " + e.args[0])
```

10. The next block of code is going to do create a SearchCursor against the GridIndexFeatures feature class for the purpose of retrieving the extent of each feature in the index layer. A SearchCursor object is a read-only copy of a feature class that is placed into memory for the explicit purpose of retrieving geometry and attribute information about the feature class. The extent object returned through the SearchCursor will then be used to pan the MapFrame. In a later step we'll then export the layout view based on the new extent.

```
import arcpy
import os

try:
    aprx = arcpy.mp.ArcGISProject(r"c:\Student\
```

```
            ProgrammingPro\Chapter6\MapSeries\MapSeries.aprx")
       arcpy.env.workspace = r"C:\Student\ProgrammingPro\
       Databases\MapBook.gdb"

       outDir = r"C:\Student\ProgrammingPro\Chapter6"
       finalpdf_filename = outDir + r"\MapSeries.pdf"
       if os.path.exists(finalpdf_filename):
           os.remove(finalpdf_filename)
       finalPdf = arcpy.mp.PDFDocumentCreate(finalpdf_filename)

       # Add the title page to the pdf
       print("Adding the title page  \n")
       finalPdf.appendPages(outDir + r"\TitlePage.pdf")

       #Add the index map to the pdf
       print("Adding the index page  \n")
       finalPdf.appendPages(outDir + r"\MapIndex.pdf")

       with arcpy.da.SearchCursor("GridIndexFeatures",
       ["PageName", "SHAPE@"], sql_clause=(None, 'ORDER
       BY PageName ASC')) as cursor:
           for row in cursor:
               print(row[0])
               lyt = aprx.listLayouts()[0]
               mf = lyt.listElements('MAPFRAME_ELEMENT',
               "Detail Map Map Frame")[0]
               mf.panToExtent(row[1].extent)

   except Exception as e:
       print("Error: " + e.args[0])
```

11. Create a new temporary PDF file for the current map in the series using the exportToPDF() method that will contain the map after it has been panned to the new extent.

```
import arcpy
import os

try:
    aprx = arcpy.mp.ArcGISProject(r"c:\Student\
    ProgrammingPro\Chapter6\MapSeries\MapSeries.aprx")
```

```python
arcpy.env.workspace = r"C:\Student\ProgrammingPro\
Databases\MapBook.gdb"

outDir = r"C:\Student\ProgrammingPro\Chapter6"
finalpdf_filename = outDir + r"\MapSeries.pdf"
if os.path.exists(finalpdf_filename):
    os.remove(finalpdf_filename)
finalPdf = arcpy.mp.PDFDocumentCreate(finalpdf_filename)

# Add the title page to the pdf
print("Adding the title page  \n")
finalPdf.appendPages(outDir + r"\TitlePage.pdf")

#Add the index map to the pdf
print("Adding the index page  \n")
finalPdf.appendPages(outDir + r"\MapIndex.pdf")

with arcpy.da.SearchCursor("GridIndexFeatures",
["PageName", "SHAPE@"], sql_clause=(None, 'ORDER
BY PageName ASC')) as cursor:
    for row in cursor:
        print(row[0])
        lyt = aprx.listLayouts()[0]
        mf = lyt.listElements('MAPFRAME_ELEMENT',
        "Detail Map Map Frame")[0]
        mf.panToExtent(row[1].extent)

        print("Creating the map series page \n")
        temp_filename = outDir + r"\tempMS.pdf"
        if os.path.exists(temp_filename):
            os.remove(temp_filename)

        lyt.exportToPDF(temp_filename)

except Exception as e:
    print("Error: " + e.args[0])
```

12. Append the map to the final PDF file. This final PDF will be a multi-page PDF document that contains one page for each map in the series along with the title and overview map pages.

```python
import arcpy
import os

try:
    aprx = arcpy.mp.ArcGISProject(r"c:\Student\
    ProgrammingPro\Chapter6\MapSeries\MapSeries.aprx")
    arcpy.env.workspace = r"C:\Student\ProgrammingPro\
    Databases\MapBook.gdb"

    outDir = r"C:\Student\ProgrammingPro\Chapter6"
    finalpdf_filename = outDir + r"\MapSeries.pdf"
    if os.path.exists(finalpdf_filename):
        os.remove(finalpdf_filename)
    finalPdf = arcpy.mp.PDFDocumentCreate(finalpdf_filename)

    # Add the title page to the pdf
    print("Adding the title page  \n")
    finalPdf.appendPages(outDir + r"\TitlePage.pdf")

    #Add the index map to the pdf
    print("Adding the index page  \n")
    finalPdf.appendPages(outDir + r"\MapIndex.pdf")

    with arcpy.da.SearchCursor("GridIndexFeatures",
    ["PageName", "SHAPE@"], sql_clause=(None, 'ORDER
    BY PageName ASC')) as cursor:
        for row in cursor:
            print(row[0])
            lyt = aprx.listLayouts()[0]
            mf = lyt.listElements('MAPFRAME_ELEMENT',
            "Detail Map Map Frame")[0]
            mf.panToExtent(row[1].extent)

            print("Creating the map series page \n")
            temp_filename = outDir + r"\tempMS.pdf"
            if os.path.exists(temp_filename):
                os.remove(temp_filename)

            lyt.exportToPDF(temp_filename)

            print("Appending the map series  \n")
```

```
                    finalPdf.appendPages(temp_filename)

        except Exception as e:
            print("Error: " + e.args[0])
```

13. Update the PDF document properties to use thumbs and a single page view. Make sure to save and close the file as well. These two lines of codes should line up to the with statement that created the SearchCursor.

```
import arcpy
import os

try:
    aprx = arcpy.mp.ArcGISProject(r"c:\Student\
    ProgrammingPro\Chapter6\MapSeries\MapSeries.aprx")
    arcpy.env.workspace = r"C:\Student\ProgrammingPro\
    Databases\MapBook.gdb"

    outDir = r"C:\Student\ProgrammingPro\Chapter6"
    finalpdf_filename = outDir + r"\MapSeries.pdf"
    if os.path.exists(finalpdf_filename):
        os.remove(finalpdf_filename)
    finalPdf = arcpy.mp.PDFDocumentCreate(finalpdf_filename)

    # Add the title page to the pdf
    print("Adding the title page  \n")
    finalPdf.appendPages(outDir + r"\TitlePage.pdf")

    #Add the index map to the pdf
    print("Adding the index page  \n")
    finalPdf.appendPages(outDir + r"\MapIndex.pdf")

    with arcpy.da.SearchCursor("GridIndexFeatures",
    ["PageName", "SHAPE@"], sql_clause=(None, 'ORDER
    BY PageName ASC')) as cursor:
        for row in cursor:
            print(row[0])
            lyt = aprx.listLayouts()[0]
            mf = lyt.listElements('MAPFRAME_ELEMENT',
            "Detail Map Map Frame")[0]
            mf.panToExtent(row[1].extent)
```

```
            print("Creating the map series page \n")
            temp_filename = outDir + r"\tempMS.pdf"
            if os.path.exists(temp_filename):
                os.remove(temp_filename)

            lyt.exportToPDF(temp_filename)

            print("Appending the map series  \n")
            finalPdf.appendPages(temp_filename)

        finalPdf.updateDocProperties(pdf_open_view="USE_THUMBS",
        pdf_layout="SINGLE_PAGE")
        finalPdf.saveAndClose()

    except Exception as e:
        print("Error: " + e.args[0])
```

14. Remove the final temporary file that contains the last map in the series.

```
import arcpy
import os

try:
    aprx = arcpy.mp.ArcGISProject(r"c:\Student\
    ProgrammingPro\Chapter6\MapSeries\MapSeries.aprx")
    arcpy.env.workspace = r"C:\Student\ProgrammingPro\
    Databases\MapBook.gdb"

    outDir = r"C:\Student\ProgrammingPro\Chapter6"
    finalpdf_filename = outDir + r"\MapSeries.pdf"
    if os.path.exists(finalpdf_filename):
        os.remove(finalpdf_filename)
    finalPdf = arcpy.mp.PDFDocumentCreate(finalpdf_filename)

    # Add the title page to the pdf
    print("Adding the title page  \n")
    finalPdf.appendPages(outDir + r"\TitlePage.pdf")

    #Add the index map to the pdf
    print("Adding the index page  \n")
    finalPdf.appendPages(outDir + r"\MapIndex.pdf")
```

```
with arcpy.da.SearchCursor("GridIndexFeatures",
["PageName", "SHAPE@"], sql_clause=(None, 'ORDER
BY PageName ASC')) as cursor:
    for row in cursor:
        print(row[0])
        lyt = aprx.listLayouts()[0]
        mf = lyt.listElements('MAPFRAME_ELEMENT',
        "Detail Map Map Frame")[0]
        mf.panToExtent(row[1].extent)

        print("Creating the map series page \n")
        temp_filename = outDir + r"\tempMS.pdf"
        if os.path.exists(temp_filename):
            os.remove(temp_filename)

        lyt.exportToPDF(temp_filename)

        print("Appending the map series  \n")
        finalPdf.appendPages(temp_filename)

    finalPdf.updateDocProperties(pdf_open_view="USE_THUMBS",
    pdf_layout="SINGLE_PAGE")
    finalPdf.saveAndClose()

    # remove the temporary data driven pages file
    if os.path.exists(temp_filename):
        print("Removing the temporary map series file")
        os.remove(temp_filename)

except Exception as e:
    print("Error: " + e.args[0])
```

15. You can check your code against a solution file found at `c:\Student\ ProgrammingPro\Solutions\Scripts\CreateMapSeries.py`

16. Run the script and it should generate some output messages similar to what you see below.

```
D4
Creating the map series page
```

```
Appending the map series

D5
Creating the map series page

Appending the map series

D6
Creating the map series page

Appending the map series

Removing the temporary map series file
```

17. Find the output file called `MapSeries.pdf` found in the `c:\Student\ProgrammingPro\Chapter6` folder and open it. Your file should appear as seen in the screenshot below.

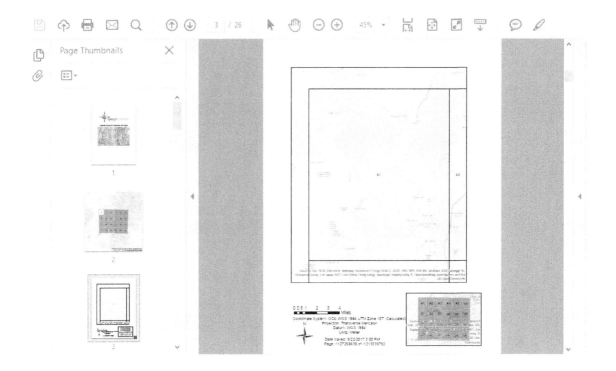

In conclusion...

The `PDFDocument` class in the `arcpy.mp` module is frequently used to create map books. In this exercise we used the `PDFDocumentCreate()` function to create an instance of `PDFDocument`. A path to the output PDF file was passed into the `PDFDocumentCreate()` function. We called the `PDFDocument.appendPages()` method twice, inserting the title page and overview map file that already existed as individual PDF files. Next, we looped through each feature in the index layer, panned the map to the extent of each feature, and exported the layout view to a temporary PDF file that was then joined to the final PDF file to create a multi-page PDF file that contains the title pages, overview map page, and individual maps.

## Chapter 7

Updating and Fixing Data Sources

In this we'll cover the following topics:

- Creating a list of broken data sources
- Fixing broken data sources

Data sources often need to be repaired or redirected to different locations due to data being moved, deleted, or changing type. These data sources are often saved in multiple projects so this isn't something you want to try to do manually. Instead, you can use the `arcpy mapping` module to accomplish this programmatically without having to manually open any project files. The `listBrokenDataSources()` method, found on the `ArcGISProject`, `LayerFile`, and `Map` classes can be used to return a list of broken data sources that are contained within these structures.

The `ArcGISProject`, `Layer`, `LayerFile`, `Map`, and `Table` classes all include an `updateConnectionProperties()` method for programmatically repairing or redirected a data source. The `Layer` and `Table` classes also include a `connectionProperties` property that can be used.

Exercise 1: Getting a list of broken data sources

Getting ready

Broken data sources are a common problem in ArcGIS Pro projects, and are typically caused by data being moved to a new location, data being deleted, or the data workspace type changing. A layer or table is indicated as broken through the use of a red exclamation point just to the side of the dataset. There are a few ways that you can repair these broken data sources using the `arcpy mapping` module. The `ArcGISProject.listBrokenDataSources()` function can be used to identify any layers in a project that are broken, and then you can apply a fix to these individual layers.

The `ArcGISProject`, `Map`, and `LayerFile` classes includes a `listBrokenDataSources()` method that returns a Python list of `Layer` and/or `Table` objects that have broken connections to their original source data. In this exercise you'll learn how to use the `listBrokenDataSources()` function to gather a list of broken datasets in a project.

How to do it...

1. Open ArcGIS Pro and create a new blank project from the `Blank.aprx` template. Call the project `Crime_BrokenDataLinks.aprx` and save it in the `c:\Student\ProgrammingPro\My Projects` folder.

2. You're going to import an existing map document file created with ArcGIS Desktop for this exercise. With the project now open, select **Import Map** from the **Insert** tab. Navigate to `c:\Student\ProgrammingPro` and select `Crime_BrokenDataLinks.mxd` and click **OK** to import the map document to the project.

3. This will import several new `Map` objects including `Crime`, `Crime_Inset`, `Inset_Map`, and `Test_Performance`. Each will have a number of layers that are broken as seen in the screenshot below.

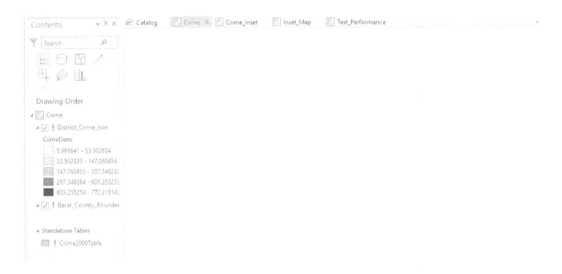

4. Open PyCharm

5. Select **File | New | Python File**.

6. Name the file `BrokenDataSources` and click **OK**. The file should be written to your default project location of `c:\Student\ProgrammingPro\Scripts` folder.

7. Import the `arcpy mapping` module, set up a basic `try/except` structure, and get a reference to the `CURRENT` project.

8. Call the `ArcGISProject.listBrokenDataSources()` method to return a list of broken data sources in the project. Print out the layer names.

```
import arcpy.mp as map
try:
    aprx = map.ArcGISProject("CURRENT")
    lyrs = aprx.listBrokenDataSources()
    for lyr in lyrs:
        print(lyr.name)

except Exception as e:
    print("Error: " + e.args[0])
```

9. You can check your code against a solution file found at `c:\Student\ProgrammingPro\Solutions\Scripts\BrokenDataSources.py`

10. Load the script into the `Crime_BrokenDataLinks.aprx` project in the ArcGIS Pro Python window and run it. You should see the list of layers printed out as seen below.

```
District_Crime_Join
Bexar_County_Boundary
Crime2009Table
School_Districts
Crime_surf
Bexar_County_Boundary
Bexar_County_Boundary
Texas_Counties_LowRes
District_Crime_Join
Bexar_County_Boundary
```

11. The `Map` and `LayerFile` objects also includes a `listBrokenDataSources()` method as well. Update your code as seen below to learn how to generate a list of broken data sources from a map instead of the project.

```
import arcpy.mp as map

try:
    aprx = map.ArcGISProject("CURRENT")
```

```
m = aprx.listMaps("Crime*")[0]
for lyr in m.listBrokenDataSources():
    print(lyr.name)
#lyrs = aprx.listBrokenDataSources()
#for lyr in lyrs:
#    print(lyr.name)

except Exception as e:
    print("Error: " + e.args[0])
```

12. Load and run the script in the ArcGIS Pro Python window. When you run this script it should print the output seen below.

```
District_Crime_Join
Bexar_County_Boundary
Crime2009Table
```

In conclusion...

The `ArcGISProject`, `Map`, and `LayerFile` objects all include a list function that generates a list of broken data sources. It's common to generate this list and then iterate the items in the list and apply a fix to each of the objects that are broken.

Exercise 2: Fixing broken data sources

Getting ready

Chances are that if you have a broken data source in one project it is also broken in other projects, as it is common to reference the same workspace only to have that location of that workspace change at some point in time. Fixing these broken data sources can be automated through a Python script that takes advantage of functions designed to apply fixes at the project, layer, layerfile, map or table levels.

The `updateConnectionProperties()` method is available on the `ArcGISProject`, `Layer`, `LayerFile`, `Map`, and `Table` classes. It's used to replace current (old) connection information with new connection information. The connection information can be provided as a partial string or a Python dictionary data structure that represents a layer or table connection properties. Although it can be used against individual layers or tables it is most useful for updating multiple data sources found in a project, layer file or map.

How to do it...

1. In ArcGIS Pro open the `Crime_BrokenDataLinks.aprx` and open Crime Map.

2. Right click the District_Crime_Join layer and select Properties.

3. Click Source on the left hand side of the dialog box and find the Database entry on the right hand side. This is the path to the current connection information, which is now broken. You can use your mouse to double click on the database entry, select it, and copy the path.

4. Return to the `BokenDataSources.py` script in PyCharm and update your code as seen below. The `updateConnectionProperties()` method takes two required parameters: the old connection path, and the new connection path. You'll also need to call the `save()` method on the `ArcGISProject` object to save the changes.

```python
import arcpy.mp as map

try:
    aprx = map.ArcGISProject("CURRENT")
    aprx.updateConnectionProperties(
        r"C:\Student\ProgrammingPro\Databases\Data\OldData\CityOfSanAn tonio.gdb",
        "C:\Student\ProgrammingPro\Databases\CityOfSanAntonio.gdb")
    aprx.save()
    #m = aprx.listMaps("Crime*")[0]
    #for lyr in m.listBrokenDataSources():
```

```
#    print(lyr.name)
#lyrs = aprx.listBrokenDataSources()
#for lyr in lyrs:
#    print(lyr.name)

except Exception as e:
    print("Error: " + e.args[0])
```

5. Load the script in the ArcGIS Pro Python window and run it. Examine each of the Map objects and the layers should now be updated as seen in the screenshot below.

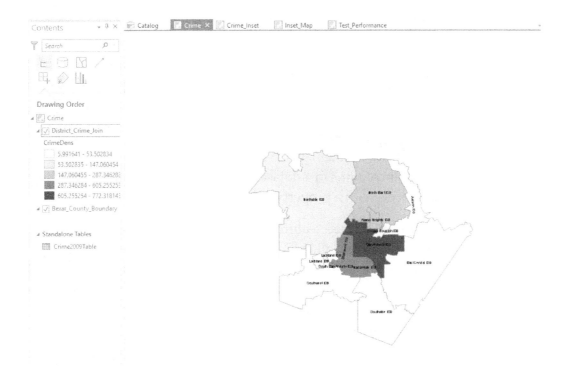

6. You can also update a data source for individual Layers and Tables using the updateConnectionProperties() method on each of these objects.

In conclusion...

The updateConnectionProperties() method can be used to fix the data connection for individual layers and tables.

## Chapter 8

Querying and Selecting Data

In this chapter you'll learn the following about querying and selecting data:

* Creating feature layers and table views
* Selecting features and rows with the Select Layer by Attribute tool
* Selecting features with the Select by Location tool
* Combining spatial and attribute queries

Selecting features from a geographic layer or rows from a stand alone attribute table is one of the most common GIS operations. Queries are created to enable these selections and can be either attribute or spatial queries. You can also combine attribute and spatial queries.

Attribute queries use SQL statements to select features or rows through the use of one or more fields or columns in a dataset. An example attribute query would be "Select all land parcels with a property value greater than $500,000".

Spatial queries are used to select features based on some type of spatial relationship. An example might be "Select all land parcels that intersect a 100 year floodplain" or perhaps "Select all streets that are completely within Travis County, Texas. It is also possible to combine attribute and spatial queries. An example might be "Select all land parcels that intersect the 100 year floodplain and have a property value greater than $500,000".

Exercise 1: Creating feature layers and table views

Getting ready

Python scripts that use the **Select Layer by Attributes** or **Select by Location** tool require that you create an intermediate dataset rather than using feature classes or tables. These intermediate datasets are temporary in nature and are called feature layers or table views. Unlike feature classes and tables, these temporary datasets do not represent actual files within a geodatabase. Instead, they are 'in memory' representations of feature classes and tables. These datasets are only active while a Python script is running. They are removed from memory after the tool has executed. However, if the script is run from within ArcGIS as a script tool the temporary layer can be saved.

The **MakeFeatureLayer** tool is used to create a feature layer that can be used as input to the **Select by Location** and **Select by Attributes** tools.

How to do it...

1. Open ArcGIS Pro and create a new project from the `Map.aptx` template. You can give the project any name you'd like and store it wherever you'd like as well. It should have only a `Topographic` basemap.

2. Open PyCharm

3. Select File | New | Python File.

4. Name the file `CreateFeatureLayer` and click OK. The file should be written to your default project location of `c:\Student\ProgrammingPro\Scripts` folder.

5. Import the `arcpy` module and set up a basic `try/except` structure. Also, set the current workspace to the `CityOfSanAntonio` geodatabase.

   ```
   import arcpy
   arcpy.env.workspace = "C:/Student/ProgrammingPro/
   Databases/CityOfSanAntonio.gdb"
   try:

   except Exception as e:
       print("Error: " + e.args[0])
   ```

6. Call the `MakeFeatureLayer` tool with the `Burglary` layer provided as the input feature class and `Burglary_Layer` the output feature layer.

   ```
   import arcpy
   arcpy.env.workspace = "C:/Student/ProgrammingPro/
   Databases/CityOfSanAntonio.gdb"
   try:
       flayer = arcpy.MakeFeatureLayer_management
       ("Burglary","Burglary_Layer")

   except Exception as e:
       print("Error: " + e.args[0])
   ```

7. You can check your code against a solution file found at `c:\Student\ProgrammingPro\Solutions\Scripts\CreateFeatureLayer.py`

8. Open the ArcGIS Pro Python window, load the script, and run it. You should see a new layer called `Burglary_Layer` added to the **Contents** pane. This is a feature layer that has been temporarily created and added to the display. It can then be used to facilitate the selection of features using the `SelectLayerByAttribute` or `SelectByLocation` tools. Unless you specifically save this layer it will be deleted at the end of your current ArcGIS Pro session.

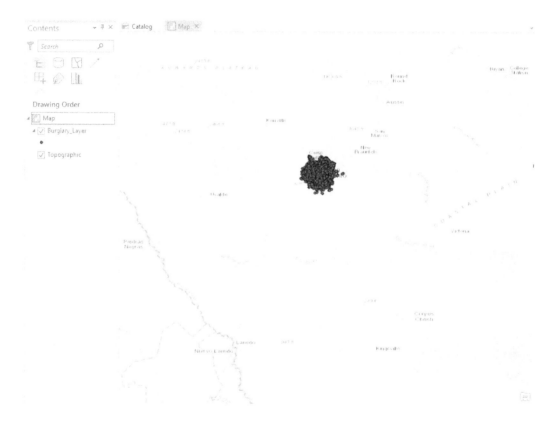

9. Return to the `CreateFeatureLayer.py` script and make the following change to create a table view instead of a feature layer.

```
import arcpy
arcpy.env.workspace = "C:/Student/ProgrammingPro/
Databases/CityOfSanAntonio.gdb"
try:
```

```
#flayer = arcpy.MakeFeatureLayer_management
("Burglary","Burglary_Layer")
tView = arcpy.MakeTableView_management
("Crime2009Table", "Crime2009TView")

except Exception as e:
    print("Error: " + e.args[0])
```

10. Load and run the script in the ArcGIS Pro Python window and you should see a new table view called `Crime2009TView` added to the Contents pane.

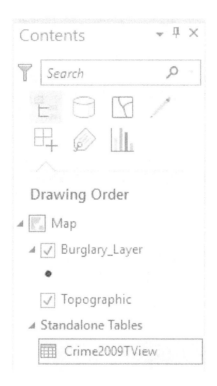

In conclusion...

Feature layers and table views are temporary, intermediate datasets used for the explicit purpose of facilitating the creation of selection sets using the **Select by Location** and **Select by Attributes** tools. In the next exercise you'll learn how to use these temporary datasets to create a selection set using the **Select Layer by Attributes** tool.

Exercise 2: Selecting features and rows with the Select Layer by Attribute tool

Getting ready

The **Select Layer by Attributes** tool is used to select records from a feature class or table based on a query that you define. In the last exercise you learned how to create a temporary, in-memory representation of a feature class or table, which is a pre-requisite to using either the **Select Layer by Attributes** or **Select by Location** tool. This tool can be used to query either a feature class or a table and does require the use of a properly constructed query.

The **Select Layer by Attributes** tool requires a feature layer or table along with a properly constructed attribute query to create a selection set. The **MakeFeatureLayer** or **MakeTableView** tool will be called first to create the temporary dataset that will be passed into the **Select Layer by Attributes** tool. A properly constructed attribute query including the field name(s) to be queried along with the value to be evaluated must also be passed as a parameter into the tool.

How to do it...

1. Open PyCharm

2. Select File | New | Python File.

3. Name the file `SelectLayerByAttribute` and click **OK**. The file should be written to your default project location of `c:\Student\ProgrammingPro\Scripts` folder.

4. Import the `arcpy` module, set up a basic `try/except` structure, and set the current workspace to the `CityOfSanAntonio` geodatabase.

5. Create the query below. This will serve as a where clause that will select all the records with a service area of `North`. In an attribute query the field to queried must be surrounded by quotes. In this case that is the `SVCAREA` field.

    If the field being queried is a `Text` datatype field, which is the case here, the value being evaluated must also be surrounded by quotes, and the quotes must be embedded inside the query. The way this is accomplished in Python is to use a \ '

both before and after the value being evaluated. This specifies that the quotes will be inserted into the where clause of the query.

Finally, the entire statement must be surrounded by quotes as well. Because there are so many quotes that need to used in an attribute query it makes sense to use a combination of single and double quotes just to make your code more readable.

```
import arcpy
arcpy.env.workspace = "C:/Student/ProgrammingPro/
Databases/CityOfSanAntonio.gdb"
try:
    qry = '"SVCAREA" = \'North\''

except Exception as e:
    print("Error: " + e.args[0])
```

6. Create a feature layer with the `MakeFeatureLayer` tool from the `Burglary` feature class.

```
import arcpy
arcpy.env.workspace = "C:/Student/ProgrammingPro/
Databases/CityOfSanAntonio.gdb"
try:
    qry = '"SVCAREA" = \'North\''
    flayer = arcpy.MakeFeatureLayer_management
    ("Burglary","Burglary_Layer")

except Exception as e:
    print("Error: " + e.args[0])
```

7. Call the `SelectLayerByAttribute` tool by passing in a reference to the feature layer you just created along with the query you defined earlier, and a constant that defines this as a new selection set.

```
import arcpy
arcpy.env.workspace = "C:/Student/ProgrammingPro/
Databases/CityOfSanAntonio.gdb"
try:
    qry = '"SVCAREA" = \'North\''
    flayer = arcpy.MakeFeatureLayer_management
    ("Burglary","Burglary_Layer")
    arcpy.SelectLayerByAttribute_management
```

```
(flayer, "NEW_SELECTION", qry)

    except Exception as e:
        print("Error: " + e.args[0])
```

8. Get a count of the number of features selected and print it out.

```
import arcpy
arcpy.env.workspace = "C:/Student/ProgrammingPro/
Databases/CityOfSanAntonio.gdb"
try:
    qry = '"SVCAREA" = \'North\''
    flayer = arcpy.MakeFeatureLayer_management
    ("Burglary","Burglary_Layer")
    arcpy.SelectLayerByAttribute_management
    (flayer, "NEW_SELECTION", qry)
    cnt = arcpy.GetCount_management(flayer)
    print("The number of selected records is: " + str(cnt))
except Exception as e:
    print("Error: " + e.args[0])
```

9. You can check your code against a solution file found at `c:\Student\ProgrammingPro\Solutions\Scripts\SelectLayerAttribute.py`

10. Typically we think of a selection set as being a visible operation performed in ArcGIS Pro where the features that have been selected are symbolized differently. However, a script that creates a selection set does not have to be run directly inside ArcGIS Pro. It can also be run from a stand-alone script. To see this in action, run the `SelectLayerAttribute.py` script from PyCharm. If everything has been done correctly you should see a message indicating that 7520 records have been selected.

```
The number of selected records is: 7520
```

In conclusion...

The creation of a selection set using the **Select by Location** or **Select Layer by Attributes** tool requires an input feature layer or table view along with a properly constructed attribute query in the case of the **Select Layer by Attributes** tool.

Exercise 3: Selecting features with the Select by Location Tool

Getting ready

The **Select by Location** tool can be used to select features based on some type of spatial relationship. Since it deals with spatial relationships this tool only applies to feature classes and their corresponding in-memory feature layers. There are many different types of spatial relationships that you can apply in the selection of features including intersect, contains, within, boundary touches, is identical, and many others. If not specified the default intersect spatial relationship will be applied. The input feature layer is the only required parameter, but there are a number of optional parameters including the spatial relationship, search distance, a feature layer or feature class to test against the input layer, and a selection type.

How to do it...

1. Open PyCharm

2. Select File | New | Python File.

3. Name the file `SelectByLocation` and click **OK**. The file should be written to your default project location of `c:\Student\ProgrammingPro\Scripts` folder.

4. Import the `arcpy` module, set up a basic `try/except` structure, and set the current workspace to the `CityOfSanAntonio` geodatabase.

5. Create a feature layer from the `Burglary` feature class.

```
import arcpy
arcpy.env.workspace = "C:/Student/ProgrammingPro/
Databases/CityOfSanAntonio.gdb"
try:
    flayer = arcpy.MakeFeatureLayer_management
    ("Burglary", "Burglary_Layer")

except Exception as e:
    print("Error: " + e.args[0])
```

6. Call the `SelectLayerbyLocation` tool, passing in a reference to the feature layer you just created. The spatial relationship test will be `COMPLETELY_WITHIN`, meaning that we want to find all burglaries that are completely within the boundaries of the comparison layer. Define `EdgewoodSD` as the comparison layer.

Also, get a count of the number of features selected and print it out.

```
import arcpy
arcpy.env.workspace = "C:/Student/ProgrammingPro/Databases/
CityOfSanAntonio.gdb"
try:
    flayer = arcpy.MakeFeatureLayer_management
    ("Burglary", "Burglary_Layer")

    arcpy.SelectLayerByLocation_management
    (flayer, "COMPLETELY_WITHIN", "EdgewoodSD")

    cnt = arcpy.GetCount_management(flayer)
    print("The number of selected records is: " + str(cnt))

except Exception as e:
    print("Error: " + e.args[0])
```

7. You can check your code against a solution file found at `c:\Student\ProgrammingPro\Solutions\Scripts\SelectByLocation.py`

8. Run the script. If everything was done correctly, you should see a message indicating that `1470` records have been selected.

   ```
   The number of selected records is: 1470
   ```

9. In the last example we did not define the optional search distance and select type parameters. By default, a new selection will be applied as the selection type. We didn't apply a distance parameter in this case, but we'll do this in the next step to illustrate how it works. Update the line of code that calls the `SelectLayerByLocation` tool as seen below.

   ```
   arcpy.SelectLayerByLocation_management (flayer,
   "WITHIN_A_DISTANCE", "EdgewoodSD","1 MILES")
   ```

10. Run the script again in PyCharm. You should now see a message indicating that `2976` records have been selected. This will select all burglaries within one mile of the boundary.

    ```
    The total number of selected records is 2976
    ```

11. The final thing you'll do in this exercise is use the `CopyFeatures` tool to write the temporary layer to a new feature class. Comment out the two lines of code that get a count of the number of features and print them to the screen.

```
#cnt = arcpy.GetCount_management(flayer)
#print("The number of selected records is: " + str(cnt))
```

12. Add a line of code that calls the CopyFeatures tool. This line should be placed just below the line of code that calls the SelectLayerByLocation tool. The CopyFeatures tool accepts a feature layer as the first input parameter and an output feature class, which in this case will be a feature class called Edgewood_Burglaries.

```
import arcpy
arcpy.env.workspace = "C:/Student/ProgrammingPro/Databases/
CityOfSanAntonio.gdb"
try:
    flayer = arcpy.MakeFeatureLayer_management
    ("Burglary", "Burglary_Layer")

    arcpy.SelectLayerByLocation_management
    (flayer, "WITHIN_A_DISTANCE", "EdgewoodSD","1 MILES")

    arcpy.CopyFeatures_management
    (flayer, "EDGEWOOD_BURLGARIES")

    #cnt = arcpy.GetCount_management(flayer)
    #print("The number of selected records is: " + str(cnt))
except Exception as e:
    print("Error: " + e.args[0])
```

In conclusion...

The **Select by Location** tool is used to select features from a layer that meet a spatial relationship and use an input feature layer.

Exercise 4: Combining spatial and attribute queries

Getting ready

There may be times when you want to select features using a combined attribute and spatial query. For example, you might want to select all burglaries within the Edgewood school district that occurred on a Monday. Running the **Select by Location** and **Select by Attributes** tools sequentially and applying a **SUBSET SELECTION** selection type can be used to accomplish a query that has a combination of spatial and attribute components.

How to do it...

1. Open PyCharm

2. Select File | New | Python File.

3. Name the file `SpatialAttributeQuery` and click OK. The file should be written to your default project location of `c:\Student\ProgrammingPro\Scripts` folder.

4. Import the `arcpy` module, set up a basic `try/except` structure, and set the current workspace to the `CityOfSanAntonio` geodatabase.

5. Create a variable for the query and define the where clause. This query will select records where the `DOW` field is equal to `Mon`. In other words, burglaries that occurred on a Monday.

```
import arcpy
arcpy.env.workspace = "C:/Student/ProgrammingPro/
Databases/CityOfSanAntonio.gdb"
try:
    qry = '"DOW" = \'Mon\''

except Exception as e:
    print("Error: " + e.args[0])
```

6. Create the feature layer from the `Burglary` layer.

```
import arcpy
arcpy.env.workspace = "C:/Student/ProgrammingPro/
Databases/CityOfSanAntonio.gdb"
try:
    qry = '"DOW" = \'Mon\''
```

```
flayer = arcpy.MakeFeatureLayer_management
("Burglary", "Burglary_Layer")

except Exception as e:
    print("Error: " + e.args[0])
```

7. Run the `SelectLayerByLocation` tool to find all burglaries within the Edgwood School District.

```
import arcpy
arcpy.env.workspace = "C:/Student/ProgrammingPro/
Databases/CityOfSanAntonio.gdb"
try:
    qry = '"DOW" = \'Mon\''
    flayer = arcpy.MakeFeatureLayer_management
    ("Burglary", "Burglary_Layer")
    arcpy.SelectLayerByLocation_management
    (flayer, "COMPLETELY_WITHIN", "EdgewoodSD")

except Exception as e:
    print("Error: " + e.args[0])
```

8. Run the `SelectLayerByAttributes` tool to find all the burglaries that match the query we previously defined in the `qry` variable. This should be defined as a subset query.

```
import arcpy
arcpy.env.workspace = "C:/Student/ProgrammingPro/
Databases/CityOfSanAntonio.gdb"
try:
    qry = '"DOW" = \'Mon\''
    flayer = arcpy.MakeFeatureLayer_management
    ("Burglary", "Burglary_Layer")
    arcpy.SelectLayerByLocation_management
    (flayer, "COMPLETELY_WITHIN", "EdgewoodSD")
    arcpy.SelectLayerByAttribute_management
    (flayer, "SUBSET_SELECTION", qry)
except Exception as e:
    print("Error: " + e.args[0])
```

9. Get the number of features that were selected and print it out.

```
import arcpy
```

```
arcpy.env.workspace = "C:/Student/ProgrammingPro/
Databases/CityOfSanAntonio.gdb"
try:
    qry = '"DOW" = \'Mon\''
    flayer = arcpy.MakeFeatureLayer_management
    ("Burglary", "Burglary_Layer")
    arcpy.SelectLayerByLocation_management
    (flayer, "COMPLETELY_WITHIN", "EdgewoodSD")
    arcpy.SelectLayerByAttribute_management
    (flayer, "SUBSET_SELECTION", qry)
    cnt = arcpy.GetCount_management(flayer)
    print("The total number of selected records is: " + str(cnt))
except Exception as e:
    print("Error: " + e.args[0])
```

10. You can check your code against a solution file found at c:\Student\ ProgrammingPro\Solutions\Scripts\SpatialAttributeQuery.py

11. Run the script and you should see that 197 features have been selected.

```
The total number of selected features is:  197
```

In conclusion...

Using a combination of the **Select Layer by Attributes** and **Select by Location** tools run in sequence you can perform queries that have both spatial and attribute components.

## Chapter 9

Using the Arcpy Data Access Module

In this chapter, we will cover the following topics:

- Retrieving features from a feature class with `SearchCursor`
- Filtering records with a where clause
- Inserting rows with `InsertCursor`
- Updating rows with `UpdateCursor`
- Deleting rows with `UpdateCursor`
- Inserting and updating rows inside an edit session
- Using `Walk()` to navigate directories
- Using the `Describe()` function to return descriptive information about a feature class
- Using the `Describe()` function to return descriptive information about a raster image

We'll start this chapter with a basic question. What are cursors? **Cursors** are in-memory objects containing one or more rows of data from a table or feature class. Each row contains the attributes from each field in the data source, along with the geometry for each feature in the case of a feature class. Cursors allow you to search, add, insert, update, and delete data from tables and feature classes.

The `arcpy` Data Access module or `arcpy.da` contains methods that allow you to iterate through each row in a cursor. Various types of cursors can be created depending upon the needs. For example, search cursors can be created to read values from rows. Update cursors can be created to update values in rows or delete rows, and insert cursors can be created to insert new rows.

There are a number of cursor improvements that have been introduced with the `arcpy.da` module. Prior to ArcGIS Desktop 10.1, cursor performance had been notoriously slow. Now, cursors are significantly faster. Esri has estimated that `SearchCursors` are up to 30 times faster while `InsertCursors` are up to 12 times faster.

In addition to these general performance improvements, the `arcpy.da` module also provides a number of options that allow programmers to speed up processing. Rather than returning all the fields in a cursor, you can now specify that a subset of fields be returned. This increases the performance, as less data needs to be returned. The same applies to geometry. Traditionally, when accessing the geometry of a feature, the entire geometric definition would be returned. You can now use geometry tokens to return a portion of the geometry rather than the full geometry for the feature. You can also use lists and tuples rather than using rows. Also new are edit sessions and the ability to work with versions, domains, and subtypes.

There are three cursor functions in `arcpy.da`. Each returns a cursor object of the same name as the function. `SearchCursor()` creates a read-only `SearchCursor` object containing rows from a table or feature class. `InsertCursor()` creates an `InsertCursor` object that can be used to insert new records into a table or feature class. `UpdateCursor()` returns a cursor object that can be used to edit or delete records from a table or feature class. Each of these cursor objects has methods for accessing rows in the cursor. You can see the relationship between the cursor functions, the objects they create, and how they are used as follows:

Function	Object Created	Usage
`SearchCursor()`	`SearchCursor`	Read only view of data from a table or feature class
`InsertCursor()`	`InsertCursor`	Adds rows to a table or feature class
`UpdateCursor()`	`UpdateCursor`	Edit or delete rows in a table or feature class

The `SearchCursor()` function is used to return a `SearchCursor` object. This object can only be used to iterate through a set of rows returned for read-only purposes. No insertions, deletions, or updates can occur through this object. An optional `where` clause can be set to limit the rows returned.

Once you've obtained a cursor instance, it is common to iterate the records, particularly with a `SearchCursor` or `UpdateCursor`. There are some peculiarities that you need to understand about navigating the records in a cursor. Cursor navigation is forward moving only. A `for` loop is typically used to iterate the contents of cursor objects one record at a time. However, cursor objects do not provide the ability to move backward one row at a time. The `reset()` method does provide a way to "start-over" since it resets the cursor pointer to the top of the cursor.

The `InsertCursor()` function is used to create an `InsertCursor` object that allows you to programmatically add new records to feature classes and tables. To insert rows call the `insertRow()` method on this object. You can also retrieve a read-only tuple containing the field names in use by the cursor through the `fields` property. A lock is placed on the table or feature class being accessed through the cursor. It's important to always design your script in a way that releases the cursor when you are done.

The `UpdateCursor()` function can be used to create an `UpdateCursor` object that can update and delete rows in a table or feature class. As is the case with an `InsertCursor`, this function places a lock on the data while it's being edited or deleted. If the cursor is used inside a Python `with` a statement, the lock will automatically be freed after the data has been processed. This hasn't always been the case. Prior to ArcGIS Desktop 10.1, cursor locks had to be explicitly released using the `del` statement. Once an instance of `UpdateCursor` has been obtained, you can then call the `updateCursor()` method to update records in tables or feature classes and the `deleteRow()` method to delete a row.

The subject of data locks requires a little more explanation. Insert and update cursors must obtain a lock on the data source they reference. This means that no other application can concurrently access this data source. Locks are a way of preventing multiple users from changing data at the same time and thus corrupting the data. When the `InsertCursor()` and `UpdateCursor()` methods are called in your code, Python attempts to acquire a lock on the data. This lock must be released after the cursor has finished processing, so that other users running applications such as ArcGIS Pro, ArcMap or ArcCatalog can access the data sources. Otherwise, no other application will be able to access the data. Similarly, ArcGIS Pro acquires a data lock when updating or deleting data. If a data source has been locked by either of these applications, your Python code will not be able to access the data. Therefore, best practice is to close ArcGIS Pro before running any standalone Python scripts that use insert or update cursors.

In this chapter, we're going to cover the use of cursors for accessing and editing tables and feature classes.

Exercise 1: Retrieving features from a feature class with a SearchCursor

Getting ready

There are many occasions when you need to retrieve rows from a table or feature class for read-only purposes. For example, you might want to generate a list of all land parcels in a city with a value greater than $100,000. In this case, you don't have any need to edit the data. Your needs are met simply by generating a list of rows that meet some sort of criteria. A SearchCursor object contains a read-only copy of rows from a table or feature class. These objects can also be filtered through the use of a where clause so that only a subset of the dataset is returned.

The SearchCursor() function is used to return a SearchCursor object. This object can only be used to iterate through a set of rows returned for read-only purposes. No insertions, deletions, or updates can occur through this object. An optional where clause can be set to limit the rows returned. In this recipe, you will learn how to create a basic SearchCursor object on a feature class through the use of the SearchCursor() function.

The SearchCursor object contains a fields property along with a reset() method. The fields property is a read-only structure in the form of a Python tuple, containing the fields requested from the feature class or table. You are going to hear the term tuple a lot in conjunction with cursors. If you haven't covered this topic before, tuples are a Python structure for storing a sequence of data similar to Python lists. But there are some important differences between Python tuples and lists. Tuples are defined as a sequence of values inside parentheses while lists are defined as a sequence of values inside brackets. Unlike lists, tuples can't grow and shrink which can be a very good thing in some cases when you want data values to occupy a specific position each time. Such is the case with cursor objects that use tuples to store data from fields in tables and feature classes.

How to do it...

Follow these steps to learn how to retrieve rows from a table or feature class inside a SearchCursor object:

1. Open PyCharm
2. Select File | New | Python File.

3. Name the file `SearchCursor` and click **OK**. The file should be written to your default project location of `c:\Student\ProgrammingPro\Scripts` folder.

4. Import the `arcpy.da` module and set up a basic `try/except` structure. Also, set the current workspace to `c:\Student\ProgrammingPro\Databases`.

```
import arcpy.da
arcpy.env.workspace = r"c:\Student\ProgrammingPro\Databases"
try:

except Exception as e:
    print("Error: " + e.args[0])
```

5. Create a `SearchCursor` object using the `Schools` shapefile and return the `Facility` and `Name` fields.

```
import arcpy.da
arcpy.env.workspace = r"c:\Student\ProgrammingPro\Databases"
try:
    with arcpy.da.SearchCursor("Schools.shp",
    ("Facility", "Name")) as cursor:

except Exception as e:
    print("Error: " + e.args[0])
```

6. Loop through the records returned in the cursor, and print out the school name.

```
import arcpy.da
arcpy.env.workspace = r"c:\Student\ProgrammingPro\Databases"
try:
    with arcpy.da.SearchCursor("Schools.shp",
    ("Facility", "Name")) as cursor:
        for row in sorted(cursor):
            print("School name: " + row[1])
except Exception as e:
    print("Error: " + e.args[0])
```

7. You can check your code against a solution file found at `c:\Student\ProgrammingPro\Solutions\Scripts\SearchCursor_Step1.py`

8. Run the script and you should see the output as shown in the screenshot below. Please note that the text you see below is only a portion of what you'll see due to space limitations.

```
School name: ALLAN
School name: ALLISON
School name: ANDREWS
School name: BARANOFF
School name: BARRINGTON
School name: BARTON CREEK
School name: BARTON HILLS
School name: BATY
School name: BECKER
School name: BEE CAVE
```

In Conclusion...

The `with` statement, used with the `SearchCursor()` function, will create, open, and close the cursor. So, you no longer have to be concerned with explicitly releasing the lock on the cursor. The first parameter passed into the `SearchCursor()` function is a feature class, represented by the `Schools.shp` file. The second parameter is a Python tuple containing a list of fields that we want returned in the cursor. For performance reasons, it is a best practice to limit the fields returned in the cursor to only those that you need to complete the task. Here, we've specified that only the `Facility` and `Name` fields should be returned. The `SearchCursor` object is stored in a variable called `cursor`.

Inside the `with` block, we are using a Python `for` loop to cycle through each school returned. We're also using the Python `sorted()` function to sort the contents of the cursor. To access the values from a field on the row, simply use the index number of the field you want to return. In this case, we want to return the contents of the `Name` column, which will be index number `1`, since it is the second item in the tuple of field names that are returned.

Exercise 2: Filtering records using a where clause

Getting ready

By default, `SearchCursor` will contain all rows in a table or feature class. However, in many cases, you will want to restrict the number of rows returned by some sort of criteria. Applying a filter through the use of a `where` clause limits the records returned.

By default, all rows from a table or feature class will be returned when you create a `SearchCursor` object. However, in many cases, you will want to restrict the records returned. You can do this by creating a query and passing it in as a `where` clause parameter when calling the `SearchCursor()` function. In this exercise, you'll build on the script you created in the previous recipe, by adding a `where` clause that restricts the records returned.

How to do it...

Follow these steps to apply a filter to a `SearchCursor` object that restricts the rows returned from a table or feature class:

1. Open PyCharm and open the `SearchCursor.py` script.

2. Update the script by adding a `where` clause that queries the `facility` field for records that have the text `High School`:

   ```
   import arcpy.da
   arcpy.env.workspace = r"c:\Student\ProgrammingPro\Databases"
   try:
       with arcpy.da.SearchCursor("Schools.shp", ("Facility",
       "Name"), '"FACILITY" = \'HIGH SCHOOL\'') as cursor:
           for row in sorted(cursor):
               print("High School name: " + row[1])
   except Exception as e:
       print("Error: " + e.args[0])
   ```

3. Run the script. The output will now be much smaller and restricted to only those schools that are high schools:

   ```
   High School name: AKINS
   High School name: ALTERNATIVE LEARNING CENTER
   High School name: ANDERSON
   High School name: AUSTIN
   ```

```
High School name: BOWIE
High School name: CROCKETT
High School name: DEL VALLE
High School name: ELGIN
```

4. You can check your code against a solution file found at `c:\Student\ProgrammingPro\Solutions\Scripts\SearchCursor_Step2.py`

In conclusion...

We covered the creation of queries in *Chapter 8: Querying and Selecting Data*, so hopefully you now have a good grasp of how these are created along with all the rules you need to follow when coding these structures. The `where` clause parameter accepts any valid SQL query, and is used in this case to restrict the number of records that are returned.

Exercise 3: Inserting rows with an InsertCursor

Getting ready

You can insert a row into a table or feature class using an `InsertCursor` object. If you want to insert attribute values along with the new row, you'll need to supply the values in the order found in the attribute table.

The `InsertCursor()` function is used to create an `InsertCursor` object that allows you to programmatically add new records to feature classes and tables. The `insertRow()` method on the `InsertCursor` object adds a row. A row, in the form of a list or tuple, is passed into the `insertRow()` method. The values in the list must correspond to the field values defined when the `InsertCursor` object was created. Just as with the other types of cursors, you can also limit the field names returned using the second parameter of the method. This function supports geometry tokens as well.

The following code example illustrates how you can use `InsertCursor` to insert new rows into a feature class. Here, we are inserting two new wildfire points into the `California` feature class. The row values to be inserted are defined in a `list` variable. Then, an `InsertCursor` object is created, passing in the feature class and fields. Finally, the new rows are inserted into the feature class using the `insertRow()` method:

```
rowValues = [{'Bastrop','N',3000,(-105.345,32.234)),
('Ft Davis','N', 456, (-109.456,33.468))]
fc = "c:/data/wildfires.gdb/California"
fields["FIRE_NAME", "FIRE_CONTAINED", "ACRES", "SHAPE@XY"]
with arcpy.da.InsertCursor(fc, fields) as cursor:
    for row in rowValues:
        cursor.insertRow(row)
```

In this exercise, you will use `InsertCursor` to add wildfires retrieved from a text file into a point feature class. When inserting rows into a feature class, you will need to know how to add the geometric representation of a feature into the feature class. This can be accomplished using `InsertCursor` along with a `Point` object. In this exercise, we will add point features in the form of wildfire incidents to an empty point feature class. In addition, you will use Python file manipulation techniques to read the coordinate data from a text file.

How to do it...

We will be importing North American wildland fire incident data from a single day in October, 2007. This data is contained in a comma-delimited text file containing one line for each fire incident on that particular day. Each fire incident has a latitude, longitude coordinate pair separated by commas along with a confidence value. This data was derived by automated methods that use remote sensing data to derive the presence or absence of a wildfire. Confidence values can range from 0 to 100. Higher numbers represent a greater confidence that this is indeed a wildfire:

1. Open the file `c:\Student\ProgrammingPro\Databases\`
   `NorthAmericaWildfire_2007275.txt` in your favorite text editor and examine the contents. You will notice that this is a simple comma-delimited text file containing longitude and latitude values for each fire along with a confidence value. We will use Python to read the contents of this file line by line and insert new point features into the `FireIncidents` feature class located in the `c:\Student\` `ProgrammingPro\Databases\WildlandFires.gdb` geodatabase.

2. Close the file.

3. In the `WildlandFires` geodatabase is a `FireIncidents` feature class. This feature class is empty. You will add features by writing a script that reads the text file you examined earlier and inserting the point data found in the file into the `FireIncidents` feature class using an `InsertCursor` object. The `FireIncidents` feature class contains a `SHAPE` field and the confidence values will be written to the `CONFIDENCEVALUE` field.

4. Open PyCharm

5. Select File | New | Python File.

6. Name the file `InsertWildfires` and click OK. The file should be written to your default project location of `c:\Student\ProgrammingPro\Scripts` folder.

7. Import the `arcpy` module and set up a basic `try/except` structure. Also, set the current workspace to `c:\Student\ProgrammingPro\Databases\` `WildlandFires.gdb`.

```
import arcpy
try:
    arcpy.env.workspace = r"C:\Student\ProgrammingPro\
    Databases\WildlandFires.gdb"
```

```
except Exception as e:
    print("Error: " + e.args[0])
```

8. Use the Python `open()` function to open the
   `NorthAmericaWildfires_2007275.txt` file in read only mode, and read all the
   lines into a Python list structure. In this step you'll also add a `finally` block that
   will close the file when you are done reading the data.

```
import arcpy
try:
    arcpy.env.workspace = r"C:\Student\ProgrammingPro\
    Databases\WildlandFires.gdb"
    f = open(r"C:\Student\ProgrammingPro\Databases\
    NorthAmericaWildfires_2007275.txt", "r")
    lstFiles = f.readlines()

except Exception as e:
    print("Error: " + e.args[0])
finally:
    f.close()
```

9. Create an `InsertCursor` object that references the `FireIncidents` feature class
   along with the `SHAPE` field information and `CONFIDENCEVALUE` field.

```
import arcpy
try:
    arcpy.env.workspace = r"C:\Student\ProgrammingPro\
    Databases\WildlandFires.gdb"
    f = open(r"C:\Student\ProgrammingPro\Databases\
    NorthAmericaWildfires_2007275.txt", "r")
    lstFires = f.readlines()
    with arcpy.da.InsertCursor("FireIncidents",
    ("SHAPE@XY","CONFIDENCEVALUE")) as cur:

except Exception as e:
    print("Error: " + e.args[0])
finally:
    f.close()
```

10. Loop through the text file line-by-line using a `for` loop. Since the text file is
    comma-delimited, we'll use the Python `split()` function to separate each
    value into a list variable called `vals`. We'll then pull out the individual latitude,

longitude, and confidence value items and assign them to variables. Finally, we'll place these values into a list variable called rowValue, which is then passed into the insertRow() function for the InsertCursor object, and we print a message:

```
import arcpy
try:
    arcpy.env.workspace = r"C:\Student\ProgrammingPro\
    Databases\WildlandFires.gdb"
    f = open(r"C:\Student\ProgrammingPro\Databases\
    NorthAmericaWildfires_2007275.txt", "r")
    lstFires = f.readlines()
    with arcpy.da.InsertCursor("FireIncidents",
    ("SHAPE@XY","CONFIDENCEVALUE")) as cur:
    cntr = 1
    for fire in lstFires:
        if 'Latitude' in fire:
            continue
        vals = fire.split(",")
        latitude = float(vals[0])
        longitude = float(vals[1])
        confid = int(vals[2])
        rowValue = [(longitude,latitude),confid]
        cur.insertRow(rowValue)
        print("Record number " + str(cntr) + " written
        to feature class")
        cntr = cntr + 1

except Exception as e:
    print("Error: " + e.args[0])
finally:
    f.close()
```

11. You can check your code against a solution file found at c:\Student\
    ProgrammingPro\Solutions\Scripts\InsertWildfires.py

12. Run the script. You should see the output below:

```
Record number 1 written to feature class
Record number 2 written to feature class
Record number 3 written to feature class
Record number 4 written to feature class
Record number 5 written to feature class
```

```
Record number 6 written to feature class
Record number 7 written to feature class
Record number 8 written to feature class
Record number 9 written to feature class
. . . . . . .
. . . . . . .
Record number 410 written to feature class
Record number 411 written to feature class
```

13. Open ArcGIS Pro and create a new project called `Wildfires` using the `Map.aptx` template file. You can save the project to you're `My Projects` folder

14. Click the **Add Data** button and navigate to `c:\Student\ProgrammingPro\Databases\WildlandFires.gdb` and add the `FireIncidents` feature class. You should see something similar to the screenshot below.

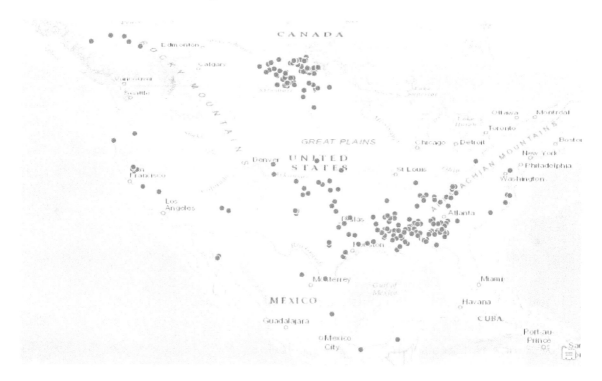

In Conclusion…

Some additional explanation may be needed here. The `lstFires` variable contains a list of all the wildfires that were contained in the comma-delimited text file. The `for` will loop through each of these records one by one, inserting each individual record into the `fire` variable. We also include an `if` statement that is used to skip the first record in the file, which serves as the header.

As I explained earlier, we then pull out the individual latitude, longitude, and confidence value items from the `vals` variable, which is just a Python list object and assign them to variables called `latitude`, `longitude`, and `confid`. We then place these values into a new list variable called `rowValue` in the order that we defined when we created `InsertCursor`. That is, the latitude and longitude pair should be placed first followed by the confidence value. Finally, we call the `insertRow()` function on the `InsertCursor` object assigned to the variable `cur`, passing in the new `rowValue` variable. We close by printing a message that indicates the progress of the script and also creating `except` and `finally` blocks to handle errors and close the text file. Placing the `file.close()` method in the `finally` block ensures that it will execute, and close the file, even if there is an error in the previous try statement.

Exercise 4: Updating rows with an UpdateCursor

Getting ready

If you need to edit or delete rows from a table or feature class, you can use `UpdateCursor`. As is the case with `SearchCursor`, the contents of `UpdateCursor` can be limited through the use of a `where` clause.

The `UpdateCursor()` function can be used to either update or delete rows in a table or feature class. The returned cursor places a lock on the data, which will automatically be released if used inside a Python `with` statement. An `UpdateCursor` object is returned from a call to this method.

The `UpdateCursor` object places a lock on the data while it's being edited or deleted. If the cursor is used inside a Python `with` statement, the lock will automatically be freed after the data has been processed. This hasn't always been the case. Previous versions of cursors required manual release using the Python `del` statement. Once an instance of `UpdateCursor` has been obtained, you can then call the `updateCursor()` method to update records in tables or feature classes and the `deleteRow()` method to delete a row.

In this exercise, you're going to write a script that updates each feature in the `FireIncidents` feature class by assigning a value of POOR, FAIR, GOOD, or EXCELLENT to a new field that is more descriptive of the confidence values using an `UpdateCursor`. Prior to updating the records, your script will add the new field to the `FireIncidents` feature class.

How to do it...

Follow these steps to create an `UpdateCursor` object that will be used to edit rows in a feature class:

1. Open PyCharm

2. Select **File | New | Python File**.

3. Name the file `UpdateWildfires` and click **OK**. The file should be written to your default project location of `c:\Student\ProgrammingPro\Scripts` folder.

4. Import the `arcpy` module and set up a basic `try/except` structure. Also, set the current workspace to `c:\Student\ProgrammingPro\Databases\`

```
WildlandFires.gdb.
    import arcpy
    try:
        arcpy.env.workspace = r"C:\Student\ProgrammingPro\
        Databases\WildlandFires.gdb"

    except Exception as e:
        print("Error: " + e.args[0])
```

5. Add a new field called CONFID_RATING to the FireIncidents feature class.
   Make sure to indent inside the try statement:

```
    import arcpy

    try:
        arcpy.env.workspace = r"C:\Student\ProgrammingPro\
        Databases\WildlandFires.gdb"
        arcpy.AddField_management("FireIncidents", "CONFID_
        RATING", "TEXT", "10")
        print("CONFID_RATING field added to FireIncidents")


    except Exception as e:
        print("Error: " + e.args[0])
```

6. Create a new instance of UpdateCursor inside a with block

```
    import arcpy

    try:
        arcpy.env.workspace = r"C:\Student\ProgrammingPro\
        Databases\WildlandFires.gdb"
        arcpy.AddField_management("FireIncidents", "CONFID_
        RATING", "TEXT", "10")
        print("CONFID_RATING field added to FireIncidents")
        with arcpy.da.UpdateCursor("FireIncidents",
        ("CONFIDENCEVALUE", "CONFID_RATING")) as cursor:


    except Exception as e:
        print("Error: " + e.args[0])
```

7. Loop through each of the rows in the `FireIncidents` fire class. Update the `CONFID_RATING` field according to the following guidelines:

- Confidence value 0 to 40 = POOR
- Confidence value 41 to 60 = FAIR
- Confidence value 61 to 85 = GOOD
- Confidence value 86 to 100 = EXCELLENT

```
import arcpy

try:
    arcpy.env.workspace = r"C:\Student\ProgrammingPro\
    Databases\WildlandFires.gdb"
    arcpy.AddField_management("FireIncidents", "CONFID_
    RATING", "TEXT", "10")
    print("CONFID_RATING field added to FireIncidents")
    with arcpy.da.UpdateCursor("FireIncidents",
    ("CONFIDENCEVALUE", "CONFID_RATING")) as cursor:
    cntr = 1
    for row in cursor:
        # update the confid_rating field
        if row[0] <= 40:
            row[1] = 'POOR'
        elif row[0] > 40 and row[0] <= 60:
            row[1] = 'FAIR'
        elif row[0] > 60 and row[0] <= 85:
            row[1] = 'GOOD'
        else:
            row[1] = 'EXCELLENT'
        cursor.updateRow(row)
        print("Record number " + str(cntr) + " updated")
        cntr = cntr + 1

except Exception as e:
    print("Error: " + e.args[0])
```

8. You can check your code against a solution file found at c:\Student\ProgrammingPro\Solutions\Scripts\UpdateWildfires.py.

9. Make sure the `FireIncidents` layer has been removed from your map in **ArcGIS Pro** before running the script. Otherwise the script won't be able to acquire a lock on the dataset.

10. Run the script. You should see messages being written to the output windows as the script runs:

```
Record number 406 updated
Record number 407 updated
Record number 408 updated
Record number 409 updated
Record number 410 updated
Record number 411 updated
```

11. Examine the `FireIncidents` feature class in **ArcGIS Pro**. Open the attribute table and you should see that a new `CONFID_RATING` field has been added and populated by the `UpdateCursor.py` script.

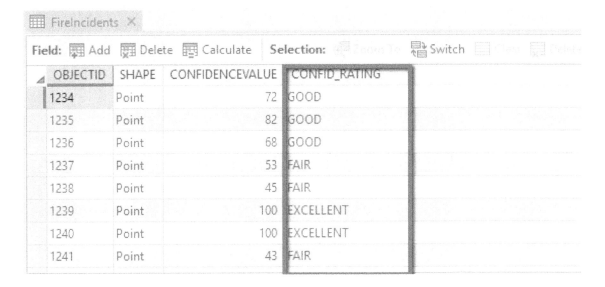

When you insert, update, or delete data in cursors, the changes are permanent and can't be undone if you're working outside an edit session. However, with edit session functionality, you can now make these changes inside an edit session to avoid these problems. We'll cover edit sessions soon.

In Conclusion...

In this case, we've used `UpdateCursor` to update each of the features in a feature class. We first used the **Add Field** tool to add a new field called `CONFID_RATING`, which will hold new values that we assign based on values found in another field. The groups are POOR, FAIR, GOOD, and EXCELLENT and are based on numeric values found in the `CONFIDENCEVALUE` field. We then created a new instance of `UpdateCursor` based on the `FireIncidents` feature class, and returned the two fields mentioned previously. The script then loops through each of the features and assigns a value of POOR, FAIR, GOOD, or EXCELLENT to the `CONFID_RATING` field (`row[1]`), based on the numeric value found in `CONFIDENCEVALUE`. A Python `if/elif/else` structure is used to control the flow of the script based on the numeric value. The value for `CONFID_RATING` is then committed to the feature class by passing in the row variable into the `updateRow()` method.

Exercise 5: Deleting rows with an UpdateCursor

Getting ready

In addition to being used to edit rows in a table or feature class, an UpdateCursor can also be used to delete rows. Please keep in mind that when rows are deleted outside an edit session, the changes are permanent.

In addition to updating records, UpdateCursor can also delete records from a table or feature class. The UpdateCursor object is created in the same way in either case, but instead of calling updateRow(), you call deleteRow() to delete a record. You can also apply a where clause to UpdateCursor, to limit the records returned. In this recipe, we'll use an UpdateCursor object that has been filtered using a where clause to delete records from our FireIncidents feature class.

How to do it...

Follow these steps to create an UpdateCursor object that will be used delete rows from a feature class:

1. Open PyCharm

2. Select File | New | Python File.

3. Name the file DeleteWildfires and click OK. The file should be written to your default project location of c:\Student\ProgrammingPro\Scripts folder.

4. Import the arcpy module and set up a basic try/except structure. Also, set the current workspace to c:\Student\ProgrammingPro\Databases\WildlandFires.gdb.

   ```
   import arcpy
   try:
       arcpy.env.workspace = r"C:\Student\ProgrammingPro\
       Databases\WildlandFires.gdb"

   except Exception as e:
       print("Error: " + e.args[0])
   ```

5. Create an UpdateCursor object for the FireIncidents feature class inside a with block.

```
try:
    arcpy.env.workspace = r"C:\Student\ProgrammingPro\
    Databases\WildlandFires.gdb"
    with arcpy.da.UpdateCursor("FireIncidents", ("CONFID_
    RATING"), 'CONFID_RATING = \'POOR\'') as cursor:


except Exception as e:
    print("Error: " + e.args[0])
```

6. Delete the returned rows by calling the `deleteRow()` method. This is done by looping through the returned cursor and deleting the rows one at a time:

```
import arcpy

try:
    arcpy.env.workspace = r"C:\Student\ProgrammingPro\
    Databases\WildlandFires.gdb"
    with arcpy.da.UpdateCursor("FireIncidents", ("CONFID_
    RATING"), 'CONFID_RATING = \'POOR\'') as cursor:
    cntr = 1
    for row in cursor:
        cursor.deleteRow()
        print("Record number " + str(cntr) + " deleted")
        cntr = cntr + 1

except Exception as e:
    print("Error: " + e.args[0])
```

7. You can check your code against a solution file found at `c:\Student\ProgrammingPro\Solutions\Scripts\DeleteWildfires.py`

8. Make sure the `FireIncidents` layer has been removed from your map in ArcGIS Pro before running the script. Otherwise the script won't be able to acquire a lock on the dataset.

9. Run the script. You should see messages being written to the output window as the script runs. 37 records should be deleted from the `FireIncidents` feature class:

```
Record number 1 deleted
Record number 2 deleted
Record number 3 deleted
```

```
Record number 4 deleted
Record number 5 deleted
```

In Conclusion...

Rows from feature classes and tables can be deleted using the deleteRow() method on UpdateCursor. In this recipe, we used a where clause in the constructor for UpdateCursor to limit the records returned to only those features with a CONFID_RATING of POOR. We then looped through the features returned in the cursor and called the deleteRow() method to delete the row from the feature class.

Exercise 6: Inserting and updating rows inside an edit session

Getting ready

As I've mentioned throughout the chapter, inserts, updates, or deletes to a table or feature class done outside an edit session are permanent. They can't be undone. Edit sessions give you much more flexibility for rolling back any unwanted changes.

Up until now, we've used insert and update cursors to add, edit, and delete data from feature classes and tables. These changes have been permanent as soon as the script was executed and can't be undone. The new `Editor` class in the Data Access module supports the ability to create edit sessions and operations. With edit sessions, changes applied to feature classes or tables are temporary until permanently applied with a specific method call.

Edit sessions begin with a call to `Editor.startEditing()`, which initiates the session. Inside the session, you then start an operation with the `Editor.startOperation()` method. From within this operation, you then perform various operations that perform edits on your data. These edits can also be subject to undo, redo, and abort operations for rolling back, rolling forward, and aborting your editing operations. After the operations have been completed, you then call the `Editor.stopOperation()` method followed by `Editor.stopEditing()`. Sessions can be ended without saving changes. In this event, changes are not permanently applied. An overview of this process is provided in the following screenshot:

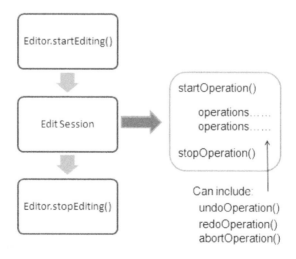

Edit sessions can also be ended without saving changes. In this event, changes are not permanently applied. Edit sessions also allow for operations to be applied inside the session and then either applied permanently to the database or rolled back. In addition, the `Editor` class also supports undo and redo operations.

The following code example shows the full edit session stack including the creation of the `Editor` object, the beginning of an edit session and an operation, edits to the data (an insert in this case), stopping the operation, and finally the end of the edit session by saving the data:

```
edit = arcpy.da.Editor('Database Connections/Portland.sde')
edit.startEditing(False)
edit.startOperation()
with arcpy.da.InsertCursor("Portland.jgp.
schools",("SHAPE","Name")) as cursor:
   cursor.insertRow([7642471.100, 686465.725), 'New School'])
edit.stopOperation()
edit.stopEditing(True)
```

The `Editor` class can be used with for file, and ArcSDE geodatabases. In addition, sessions can also be started and stopped on versioned databases. You are limited to editing only a single workspace at a time, and this workspace is specified in the constructor for the `Editor` object simply by passing in a string that references the workspace. Once created, this `Editor` object then has access to all the methods for starting, stopping, and aborting operations, and performing undo and redo operations.

How to do it...

Follow these steps to wrap `UpdateCursor` inside an edit session:

1. Open PyCharm

2. Select File | New | Python File.

3. Name the file `EditSessionUpdateWildfires` and click OK. The file should be written to your default project location of `c:\Student\ProgrammingPro\Scripts` folder.

4. Import the `arcpy` module and set up a basic `try`/`except` structure. Also, set the current workspace to `c:\Student\ProgrammingPro\Databases\WildlandFires.gdb`.

```
import arcpy
try:
    arcpy.env.workspace = r"C:\Student\ProgrammingPro\
    Databases\WildlandFires.gdb"

except Exception as e:
    print("Error: " + e.args[0])
```

5. Create an instance of the Editor class and start an edit session. These lines of code should be placed just inside the try block:

```
import arcpy

try:
    arcpy.env.workspace = r"C:\Student\ProgrammingPro\
    Databases\WildlandFires.gdb"
    edit = arcpy.da.Editor(r"C:\Student\ProgrammingPro\
    Databases\WildlandFires.gdb")
    edit.startEditing(True)


except Exception as e:
    print("Error: " + e.args[0])
```

6. Create an UpdateCursor object using a with statement:

```
import arcpy

try:
    arcpy.env.workspace = r"C:\Student\ProgrammingPro\
    Databases\WildlandFires.gdb"
    edit = arcpy.da.Editor(r"C:\Student\ProgrammingPro\
    Databases\WildlandFires.gdb")
    edit.startEditing(True)
    with arcpy.da.UpdateCursor("FireIncidents",
    ("CONFIDENCEVALUE", "CONFID_RATING")) as cursor:


except Exception as e:
    print("Error: " + e.args[0])
```

7. Loop through the records in the cursor and apply the attribute edits as seen below

```
import arcpy
```

```
try:
    arcpy.env.workspace = r"C:\Student\ProgrammingPro\
    Databases\WildlandFires.gdb"
    edit = arcpy.da.Editor(r"C:\Student\ProgrammingPro\
    Databases\WildlandFires.gdb")
    edit.startEditing(True)
    with arcpy.da.UpdateCursor("FireIncidents",
    ("CONFIDENCEVALUE", "CONFID_RATING")) as cursor:
    cntr = 1
    for row in cursor:
        # update the confid_rating field
        if row[0] > 40 and row[0] <= 60:
            row[1] = 'GOOD'
        elif row[0] > 60 and row[0] <= 85:
            row[1] = 'BETTER'
        else:
                row[1] = 'BEST'

except Exception as e:
    print("Error: " + e.args[0])
```

8. Call the updateRow() method on the UpdateCursor object and print out progress information.

```
import arcpy

try:
    arcpy.env.workspace = r"C:\Student\ProgrammingPro\
    Databases\WildlandFires.gdb"
    edit = arcpy.da.Editor(r"C:\Student\ProgrammingPro\
    Databases\WildlandFires.gdb")
    edit.startEditing(True)
    with arcpy.da.UpdateCursor("FireIncidents",
    ("CONFIDENCEVALUE", "CONFID_RATING")) as cursor:
    cntr = 1
    for row in cursor:
        # update the confid_rating field
        if row[0] > 40 and row[0] <= 60:
            row[1] = 'GOOD'
        elif row[0] > 60 and row[0] <= 85:
            row[1] = 'BETTER'
```

```
        else:
            row[1] = 'BEST'
        cursor.updateRow(row)
        print("Record number " + str(cntr) + " updated")
        cntr = cntr + 1

    except Exception as e:
        print("Error: " + e.args[0])
```

9. End the edit session and save edits. This line of code should line up to the `with` statement.

```
    import arcpy

    try:
        arcpy.env.workspace = r"C:\Student\ProgrammingPro\
        Databases\WildlandFires.gdb"
        edit = arcpy.da.Editor(r"C:\Student\ProgrammingPro\
        Databases\WildlandFires.gdb")
        edit.startEditing(True)
        with arcpy.da.UpdateCursor("FireIncidents",
        ("CONFIDENCEVALUE", "CONFID_RATING")) as cursor:
        cntr = 1
        for row in cursor:
            # update the confid_rating field
            if row[0] > 40 and row[0] <= 60:
                row[1] = 'GOOD'
            elif row[0] > 60 and row[0] <= 85:
                row[1] = 'BETTER'
            else:
                row[1] = 'BEST'
            cursor.updateRow(row)
            print("Record number " + str(cntr) + " updated")
            cntr = cntr + 1
        edit.stopEditing(True)

    except Exception as e:
        print("Error: " + e.args[0])
```

10. You can check your code against a solution file found at `c:\Student\ProgrammingPro\Solutions\Scripts\EditSessionUpdateWildfires.py`

11. Make sure the `FireIncidents` layer has been removed from your map in ArcGIS Pro before running the script. Otherwise the script won't be able to acquire a lock on the dataset.

12. Run the script. You should see messages being written to the output window as the script runs. `374` records should be updated from the `FireIncidents` feature class:

In Conclusion...

Edit operations should take place inside an edit session, which can be initiated with the `Editor.startEditing()` method. The `startEditing()` method takes two optional parameters including `with_undo` and `multiuser_mode`. The `with_undo` parameter accepts a Boolean value of `true` or `false`, with a default of `true`. This creates an undo/redo stack when set to `true`. The `multiuser_mode` parameter defaults to `true`. When `false`, you have full control of editing a non-versioned or versioned dataset. If your dataset is non-versioned and you use `stopEditing(False)`, your edit will not be committed. Otherwise, if set to `true`, your edits will be committed to the underlying dataset. The `Editor.stopEditing()` method takes a single Boolean value of `true` or `false`, indicating whether changes should be saved or not. This defaults to `true`.

The `Editor` class supports undo and redo operations. We'll first look at undo operations. During an edit session, various edit operations can be applied. In the event that you need to undo a previous operation, a call to `Editor.undoOperation()` will remove the most previous edit operation in the stack. This is illustrated as follows:

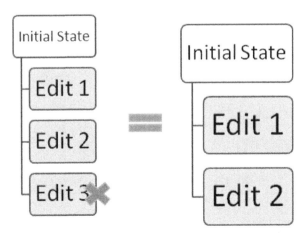

Redo operations, initiated by the `Editor.redoOperation()` method, will redo an operation that was previously undone. This is illustrated as follows:

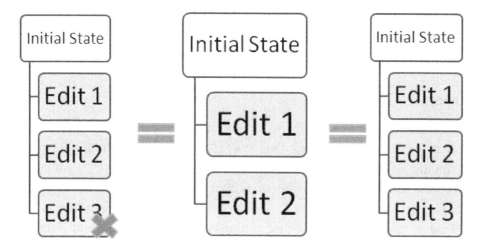

Exercise 7: Using Walk() to navigate directories

Getting ready

In this exercise you will learn how to generate data names in a catalog tree using the `arcpy.da Walk()` function. Though similar to the Python `os.walk()` function, the `da.Walk()` function provides some important enhancements related to geodatabases.

The `Walk()` function, which is part of the `arcpy.da`, module generates data names in a catalog tree by walking the tree top-down or bottom-up. Each directory or workspace yields a tuple containing the directory path, directory names, and file names. This function is similar to the Python `os.walk()` function but it has the added advantage of being able to recognize geodatabase structures. The `os.walk()` function is file based so it isn't able to tell you information about geodatabase structures while `arcpy.da.walk()` can do so.

How to do it...

Follow these steps to learn how to use the `da.Walk()` function to navigate directories and workspaces to reveal the structure of a geodatabase:

1. Open PyCharm

2. Select **File | New | Python File**.

3. Name the file `DAWalk.py` and click **OK**. The file should be written to your default project location of `c:\Student\ProgrammingPro\Scripts` folder.

4. Import the `arcpy and os` modules and set up a basic `try/except` structure. Also, set the current workspace to `c:\Student\ProgrammingPro\Databases`.

    ```
    import arcpy
    try:
        arcpy.env.workspace = r"C:\Student\ProgrammingPro\
        Databases"

    except Exception as e:
        print("Error: " + e.args[0])
    ```

5. Call the Python `os.walk()` method and print out the filenames in the current workspace.

    ```
    import arcpy
    ```

```
import os
try:
    arcpy.env.workspace = r"C:\Student\ProgrammingPro\
    Databases"
    for dirpath, dirnames, filenames in   os.walk(arcpy.
    env.workspace):
        for filename in filenames:
            print(filename)


except Exception as e:
    print("Error: " + e.args[0])
```

6. You can check your code against a solution file found at `c:\Student\ProgrammingPro\Solutions\Scripts\DAWalk.py`

7. Run the script and you should see each of the file names in the current workspace printed out. Although `os.walk()` can be used to print all file names within a directory you'll notice that it doesn't have an understanding of the structure of Esri GIS format datasets like file geodatabases. Files like `a000000001.gdbindexes` are physical files that make up a feature class but `os.walk()` can't tell you the logical structure of a feature class. In the next step we'll use `da.walk()` to resolve this problem.

```
Schools.dbf
Schools.prj
Schools.sbn
Schools.sbx
Schools.shp
Schools.shp.xml
Schools.shx
Zoning.lyrx
a00000001.freelist
a00000001.gdbindexes
a00000001.gdbtable
a00000001.gdbtablx
a00000002.gdbtable
a00000002.gdbtablx
a00000003.gdbindexes
a00000003.gdbtable
a00000003.gdbtablx
```

```
a00000004.CatItemsByPhysicalName.atx
a00000004.CatItemsByType.atx
a00000004.FDO_UUID.atx
a00000004.freelist
a00000004.gdbindexes
```

8. Update the code in the DAWalk script as seen below to use the arcpy.da.Walk() method.

```
import arcpy.da
import os
try:
    arcpy.env.workspace = r"C:\Student\ProgrammingPro\
    Databases"
    for dirpath, dirnames, filenames in arcpy.da.Walk
    (arcpy.env.workspace, datatype="FeatureClass"):
        for filename in filenames:
            print(os.path.join(dirpath,filename))

except Exception as e:
    print("Error: " + e.args[0])
```

9. You can check your code against a solution file found at c:\Student\ProgrammingPro\Solutions\Scripts\DAWalk.py

10. Run the script and now you should see the individual feature class names inside the geodatabases in addition to the shapefiles in the current workspace.

```
C:\Student\ProgrammingPro\Databases\coa_parcels.shp
C:\Student\ProgrammingPro\Databases\Schools.shp
C:\Student\ProgrammingPro\Databases\CityOfSanAntonio.gdb\
Crimes2009
C:\Student\ProgrammingPro\Databases\CityOfSanAntonio.gdb\
CityBoundaries
C:\Student\ProgrammingPro\Databases\CityOfSanAntonio.gdb\
CrimesBySchoolDistrict
C:\Student\ProgrammingPro\Databases\CityOfSanAntonio.gdb\
SchoolDistricts
C:\Student\ProgrammingPro\Databases\CityOfSanAntonio.gdb\
BexarCountyBoundaries
C:\Student\ProgrammingPro\Databases\CityOfSanAntonio.gdb\
Texas_Counties_LowRes
```

In Conclusion...

The `arcpy.da` module includes a `walk()` function that is capable of reading the internal structure of a geodatabase. This function is similar to the Python `os.walk()` function, which doesn't have the ability to understand the logical structure of a geodatabase.

Exercise 8: Using the Describe() function to return descriptive information about a feature class

Getting ready

All datasets contain information that is descriptive in nature. For example, a feature class has a name, shape type, spatial reference, extent, and so on. This information can be valuable to your scripts when you are seeking specific information before continuing with further processing in the script. For example, you might want to perform a buffer only on polyline feature classes instead of points or polygons. Using the `Describe()` function, you can obtain basic descriptive information about any dataset. You can think of this information as metadata.

The `Describe()` function provides you with the ability to get basic information about datasets. These datasets could include feature classes, tables, ArcInfo coverages, layer files, workspaces, rasters, and so on. A `Describe` object is returned and contains specific properties, based on the data type being described. Properties on the `Describe` object are organized into property groups and all datasets fall into at least one property group. For example, performing `Describe()` against a geodatabase would return the GDB `FeatureClass`, `FeatureClass`, `Table`, and `Dataset` property groups. Each of these property groups contains specific properties that can be examined.

The `Describe()` function accepts a string parameter, which is a pointer to a datasource. In the following code example, we pass a feature class that is contained within a file geodatabase. The function returns a `Describe` object that contains a set of dynamic properties called property groups. We can then access these various properties as we have done in this case by simply printing out the properties using the print function:

```
arcpy.env.workspace = r"c:\Student\ProgrammingPro\
Databases\CityOfSanAntonio.gdb"
desc = arcpy.da.Describe("Schools")
print("The feature type is: " + desc['featureType'])
```

```
The feature type is: Simple
print("The shape type is: " + desc['shapeType'])
The shape type is: Polygon
print("The name is: " + desc['name'])
The name is: Schools
print("The path to the data is: " + desc['path'])
The path to the data is: c:\Student\ProgrammingPro\
Databases\CityOfSanAntonio.gdb
```

All datasets, regardless of their type, contain a default set of properties located on the Describe object. These are read-only properties. Some of the more commonly used properties include dataType, catalogPath, name, path, and file.

In this exercise, you will write a script that obtains descriptive information about a feature class using the Describe() function.

How to do it...

Follow these steps to learn how to obtain descriptive information about a feature class.

1. Open PyCharm

2. Select File | New | Python File.

3. Name the file DescribeFeatureClass and click OK. The file should be written to your default project location of c:\Student\ProgrammingPro\Scripts folder.

4. Import the arcpy module and set up a basic try/except structure. Also, set the current workspace to c:\Student\ProgrammingPro\Databases\CityOfSanAntonio.gdb.

```
import arcpy
try:
    arcpy.env.workspace = r"C:\Student\ProgrammingPro\
    Databases\CityOfSanAntonio.gdb"

except Exception as e:
    print("Error: " + e.args[0])
```

5. Call the Describe() function on the Burglary feature class and print out the shape type:

```
import arcpy

try:
    arcpy.env.workspace = r"C:\Student\ProgrammingPro\
    Databases\CityOfSanAntonio.gdb"
    desc = arcpy.da.Describe("Burglary")
    print("The shape type is: " + desc['shapeType'])

except Exception as e:
    print("Error: " + e.args[0])
```

6. Get a list of fields in the feature class and print out the name, type, and length of each.

```
import arcpy

try:
    arcpy.env.workspace = r"C:\Student\ProgrammingPro\
    Databases\CityOfSanAntonio.gdb"
    desc = arcpy.da.Describe("Burglary")
    print("The shape type is: " + desc['shapeType'])
    for fld in desc['fields']:
        print("Field: " + fld.name)
        print("Type: " + fld.type)
        print("Length: " + str(fld.length))
except Exception as e:
    print("Error: " + e.args[0])
```

7. Get the geographic extent of the feature class and print out the coordinates that define the extent.

```
import arcpy

try:
    arcpy.env.workspace = r"C:\Student\ProgrammingPro\
    Databases\CityOfSanAntonio.gdb"
    desc = arcpy.da.Describe("Burglary")
    print("The shape type is: " + desc['shapeType'])
    for fld in desc['fields']:
        print("Field: " + fld.name)
        print("Type: " + fld.type)
        print("Length: " + str(fld.length))
```

```
    ext = desc['extent']
    print("XMin: %f" % (ext.XMin))
    print("YMin: %f" % (ext.YMin))
    print("XMax: %f" % (ext.YMin))
    print("YMax: %f" % (ext.YMax))

except Exception as e:
    print("Error: " + e.args[0])
```

8. You can check your code against a solution file found at `c:\Student\ProgrammingPro\Solutions\Scripts\DescribeFeatureClass.py`

9. Run the script and you should see a print out of the shape type, fields, and extent as seen below:

```
The shape type is: Point
Field: OBJECTID
Type: OID
Length: 4
Field: Shape
Type: Geometry
Length: 0
Field: CASE
Type: String
Length: 11
Field: LOCATION
Type: String
Length: 40
....
....
XMin: -103.518030
YMin: -6.145758
XMax: -98.243208
YMax: 29.676404
```

In conclusion...

Performing a `Describe()` against a feature class, which we have done in this script, returns a `FeatureClass` property group along with access to the `Table` and `Dataset` property groups, respectively. In addition to returning a `FeatureClass` property group, you also have access to a `Table` properties group.

The `Table` property group is important primarily because it gives you access to the fields in a standalone table or feature class. You can also access any indexes on the table or feature class through this property group. The `Fields` property in `Table` properties returns a Python list containing one `Field` object for each field in the feature class. Each field has a number of read-only properties including the `name`, `alias`, `length`, `type`, `scale`, `precision`, and so on. The most obviously useful properties are `name` and `type`. In this script, we printed out the field name, type, and length. Note the use of a Python `for` loop to process each field in the Python list.

Finally, we printed out the geographic extent of the layer through the use of the `Extent` object, returned by the `extent` property in the `Dataset` property group. The `Dataset` property group contains a number of useful properties. Perhaps the most used properties include `extent` and `spatialReference`, as many geoprocessing tools and scripts require this information at some point during execution. You can also obtain the `datasetType` and versioning information along with several other properties.

Exercise 9: Using the Describe() function to return descriptive information about a raster image

Getting ready

A raster dataset can also be described through the use of the Describe() function. In this exercise, you will describe a raster dataset by returning its extent and spatial reference. The Describe() function contains a reference to the general purpose Dataset properties group and also contains a reference to the SpatialReference object for the dataset. The SpatialReference object can then be used to get detailed spatial reference information for the dataset.

How to do it...

Follow these steps to learn how to obtain descriptive information about a raster image file.

1. Open PyCharm

2. Select File | New | Python File.

3. Name the file DescribeRaster and click OK. The file should be written to your default project location of c:\Student\ProgrammingPro\Scripts folder.

4. Import the arcpy module and set up a basic try/except structure. Also, set the current workspace to C:\Student\ProgrammingPro\Databases.

   ```
   import arcpy
   try:
       arcpy.env.workspace = r" C:\Student\ProgrammingPro\
       Databases"

   except Exception as e:
       print("Error: " + e.args[0])
   ```

5. Call the Describe() function on a raster dataset.

   ```
   import arcpy

   try:
       arcpy.env.workspace = r"C:\Student\ProgrammingPro\
       Databases"
       desc = arcpy.da.Describe("AUSTIN_EAST_NW.sid")
   ```

```
    except Exception as e:
        print("Error: " + e.args[0])
```

6. Get the extent of the raster dataset and print it out.

```
import arcpy

try:
    arcpy.env.workspace = r"C:\Student\ProgrammingPro\
    Databases"

    desc = arcpy.da.Describe("AUSTIN_EAST_NW.sid")
    ext = desc['extent']
    print("XMin: %f" % (ext.XMin))
    print("YMin: %f" % (ext.YMin))
    print("XMax: %f" % (ext.YMin))
    print("YMax: %f" % (ext.YMax))

except Exception as e:
    print("Error: " + e.args[0])
```

7. Get a reference to the SpatialReference object and print it out.

```
import arcpy

try:
    arcpy.env.workspace = r"C:\Student\ProgrammingPro\
    Databases"
    desc = arcpy.da.Describe("AUSTIN_EAST_NW.sid")

    ext = desc['extent']
    print("XMin: %f" % (ext.XMin))
    print("YMin: %f" % (ext.YMin))
    print("XMax: %f" % (ext.YMin))
    print("YMax: %f" % (ext.YMax))

    sr = desc['spatialReference']
    print(sr.name)
    print(sr.type)

except Exception as e:
    print("Error: " + e.args[0])
```

8. You can check your code against a solution file found at `c:\Student\`
   `ProgrammingPro\Solutions\Scripts\DescribeRaster.py`

9. Run the script and you should see a print out of the extent and spatial reference as seen below:

```
XMin: 3111134.862457
YMin: 10086853.262238
XMax: 10086853.262238
YMax: 10110047.019228
NAD_1983_Texas_Central
Projected
```

In conclusion...

This exercise is very similar to the previous. The difference is that we're using the `Describe()` function against a raster dataset instead of a vector feature class. In both cases, we've returned the geographic extent of the datasets using the `Extent` object. However, in the script, we've also obtained the `SpatialReference` object for the raster dataset and printed out information about this object including its name and type.

## Chapter 10

Creating Custom Geoprocessing Tools

In this chapter, we will cover the following exercises:

- Creating a custom geoprocessing tool
- Creating a Python toolbox

In addition to accessing the system geoprocessing tools provided by ArcGIS Pro, you can also create your own custom tools. These tools work in the same way that system tools do and can be used in ModelBuilder, Python window, or a standalone Python scripts. Many organizations build their own library of tools that perform geoprocessing operations specific to their data. In ArcGIS Pro there are two ways that you can create custom geoprocesisng tools: custom script tools in a custom toolbox and custom script tools in a Python toolbox. Both methods essentially accomplish the same thing, but the workflow for creating the custom tools differs significantly. We'll cover both methods in this chapter.

Exercise 1: Creating a custom geoprocessing tool

Getting ready

In this exercise, you will learn to create custom geoprocessing script tools by attaching a Python script to a custom toolbox. There are a number of advantages to creating a custom script tool. When you take this approach, the script becomes a part of the geoprocessing framework, which means that it can be run from a model, command line, or another script. In addition to this, the script has access to ArcGIS Pro environment settings and help documentation. Other advantages include a nice, easy-to-use user interface and error prevention capabilities. Error prevention capabilities provided include a dialog box that informs the user of certain errors.

These custom developed script tools must be added to a custom toolbox that you create, because the system toolboxes provided with ArcGIS Pro are read-only toolboxes and thus can't accept new tools.

In this exercise, you are going to be provided with a pre-written Python script that reads wildfire data from a comma-delimited text file, and writes this information to a point feature class called `FireIncidents`. References to these datasets have been hardcoded, so you are going to alter the script to accept dynamic variable input. You'll then attach the script to a custom tool to give your end users a visual interface for using the script.

How to do it...

The custom Python geoprocessing scripts that you write can be added to custom toolboxes. You are not allowed to add your scripts to any of the system toolboxes, such as **Analysis** or **Data Management**. However, by creating a new custom toolbox, you can add these scripts.

1. Open PyCharm

2. Select File | New | Python File.

3. Name the file `InsertWildfiresToolbox` and click OK. The file should be written to your default project location of `c:\Student\ProgrammingPro\Scripts` folder.

4. Import the `arcpy` and `os` modules and set up a basic `try/except` structure.

   ```
   import arcpy, os
   try:

   except Exception as e:
       print("Error: " + e.args[0])
   ```

5. Create variables to hold the output feature class, feature class template, and text file. Use the `arcpy.GetParameterAsText()` function to retrieve these values from the script tool dialog.

   ```
   import arcpy, os

   try:
       outputFC = arcpy.GetParameterAsText(0)
       fClassTemplate = arcpy.GetParameterAsText(1)
   ```

```
        f = open(arcpy.GetParameterAsText(2), 'r')

    except Exception as e:
        print("Error: " + e.args[0])
```

6. Create a new feature class using the input provided by the user in the first parameter.

```
import arcpy, os

try:
    outputFC = arcpy.GetParameterAsText(0)
    fClassTemplate = arcpy.GetParameterAsText(1)
    f = open(arcpy.GetParameterAsText(2), 'r')
    arcpy.CreateFeatureclass_management(
        os.path.split(outputFC)[0],
        os.path.split(outputFC)[1],
        "point",
        fClassTemplate)

except Exception as e:
    print("Error: " + e.args[0])
```

7. Read each of the lines in the text file into a Python list.

```
import arcpy, os

try:
    outputFC = arcpy.GetParameterAsText(0)
    fClassTemplate = arcpy.GetParameterAsText(1)
    f = open(arcpy.GetParameterAsText(2), 'r')
    arcpy.CreateFeatureclass_management(
        os.path.split(outputFC)[0],
        os.path.split(outputFC)[1],
        "point",
        fClassTemplate)
    lstFires = f.readlines()

except Exception as e:
    print("Error: " + e.args[0])
```

8. Defines a Python list containing the fields to be used when inserting geometry and attributes.

```
import arcpy, os

try:
    outputFC = arcpy.GetParameterAsText(0)
    fClassTemplate = arcpy.GetParameterAsText(1)
    f = open(arcpy.GetParameterAsText(2), 'r')
    arcpy.CreateFeatureclass_management(
        os.path.split(outputFC)[0],
        os.path.split(outputFC)[1],
        "point",
        fClassTemplate)
    lstFires = f.readlines()
    fields = ["SHAPE@XY", "CONFIDENCEVALUE"]

except Exception as e:
    print("Error: " + e.args[0])
```

9. Create an `InsertCursor` from the feature class, loop through each of the fires found in the text file, extract the coordinates and confidence value attributes, and insert the information into the output feature class.

```
try:
    outputFC = arcpy.GetParameterAsText(0)
    fClassTemplate = arcpy.GetParameterAsText(1)
    f = open(arcpy.GetParameterAsText(2), 'r')
    arcpy.CreateFeatureclass_management(
        os.path.split(outputFC)[0],
        os.path.split(outputFC)[1],
        "point",
        fClassTemplate)
    lstFires = f.readlines()
    fields = ["SHAPE@XY", "CONFIDENCEVALUE"]
    with arcpy.da.InsertCursor(outputFC, fields) as cur:
        for fire in lstFires:
            if 'Latitude' in fire:
                continue
            vals = fire.split(",")
            latitude = float(vals[0])
            longitude = float(vals[1])
            confid = int(vals[2])
            row_values = [(longitude, latitude), confid]
```

```
                    cur.insertRow(row_values)

   except Exception as e:
       print("Error: " + e.args[0])
```

10. You can check your code against a solution file found at `c:\Student\`
    `ProgrammingPro\Solutions\Scripts\InsertWildfiresToolbox.py`.

    Now we'll attach the script to a tool using the ArcGIS Pro interface.

11. Open ArcGIS Pro and create a new project using the `Map.aptx` template.
    Name the project `CustomWildfireTool` and save it in the `c:\Student\`
    `ProgrammingPro\My Projects` folder.

12. In the Catalog pane open the Toolboxes folder and find the
    `CustomWildfireTool.tbx` toolbox.

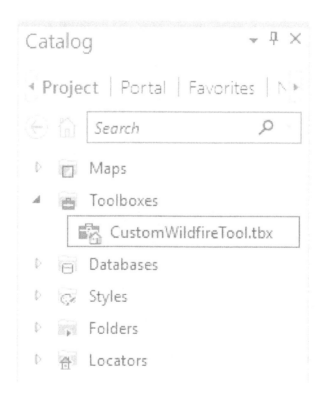

13. Right click `CustomWildfireTool.tbx` and select New | Script.

14. The General dialog will be displayed initially. Here you will enter the following parameters.

- **Name:** `InsertWildfires`
- **Label:** `Insert Wildfires`
- **Script File:** `c:\Student\ProgrammingPro\Scripts\`
  `InsertWildfiresToolbox.py`

15. Click the Parameters tab and enter the parameters seen in the screenshot below.

16. This tool won't include any custom validation so you can click **OK** to create the custom script tool seen in the screenshot below.

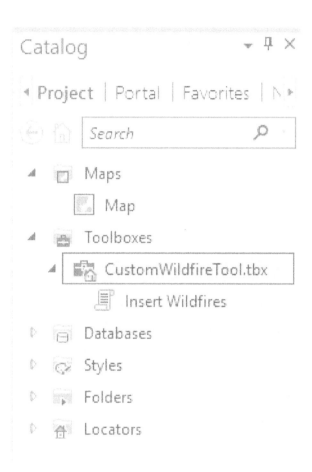

17. Before running the tool you'll need to create a connection to the geodatabase containing the `Wildfire` geodatabase. In the **Catalog** pane, Open the **Databases** folder and select **Add Database**.

18. Navigate to the `c:\Student\ProgrammingPro\Databases` folder and select `WildlandFires.gdb`.

19. Double click the InsertWildfires tool found in the CustomWildfireTool toolbox and fill in the parameters as defined below:

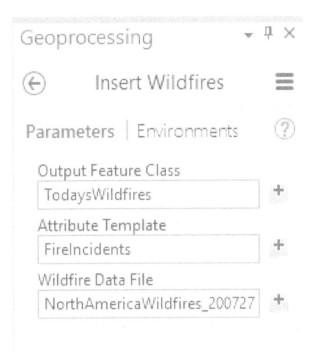

- Output Feature Class – C:\Student\ProgrammingPro\Databases\ WildlandFires.gdb\TodaysWildfires
- Attribute Template – C:\Student\ProgrammingPro\Databases\ WildlandFires.gdb\FireIncidents
- Wildfire Data File – C:\Student\ProgrammingPro\Databases\ NorthAmericaWildfires_2007275.txt

20. Click Run to execute the tool. If everything goes correctly you should see the TodaysWildfires layer added to the Contents pane.

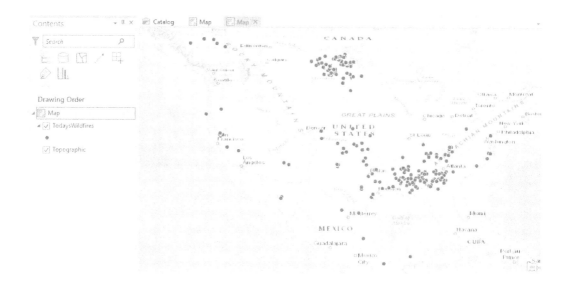

21. Open the attribute table to verify that the CONFIDENCEVALUE field has been populated.

In conclusion...

Custom script tools in a custom toolbox are used to provide a visual interface to your Python scripts. End users of these tools don't need to understand anything about Python to use the tools. They look just like every other tool in the ArcGIS Pro toolbox. These tools can be used to accomplish a wide variety of geoprocessing tasks.

Exercise 2: Creating a Python toolbox

Getting ready

There are two ways to create toolboxes in **ArcGIS Pro**: script tools in custom toolboxes that we covered in the last exercise, and script tools in Python toolboxes. Python toolboxes were introduced at version 10.1 of ArcGIS Desktop and they encapsulate everything in one place: parameters, validation code, and source code. This is not the case with custom toolboxes, which are created using a wizard and a separate script that processes the business logic.

A **Python Toolbox** functions like any other toolbox but it is created entirely in Python and has a file extension of `.pyt`. It is created programmatically as a class named `Toolbox`. In this exercise you will learn how to create a **Python Toolbox** and add a custom tool.

In this exercise you'll create a custom Python toolbox that connects to a live USGS map service that contains real time wildfire information. After creating the basic structure of the `Toolbox` and `Tool` you'll complete the functionality of the tool by adding code that connects to an **ArcGIS Server** map service, downloads real time data, and inserts it into a feature class.

How to do it...

Complete the steps below to create a **Python Toolbox** and create a custom tool that connects to an ArcGIS Server map service, downloads real time data, and inserts it into a feature class.

1. Open the CustomWildfireTool project in ArcGIS Pro and find the Toolboxes folder in the Catalog pane.

2. Right click the Toolboxes folder and select New Python Toolbox.

3. Name the toolbox RealTimeWildfireTool and place it into the Toolboxes folder for the Project as seen in the screenshot below.

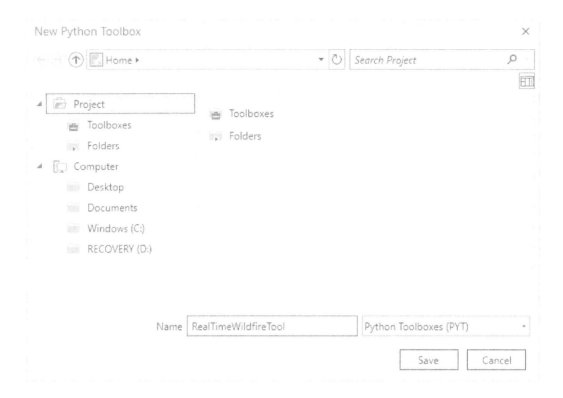

4. Click Save to create the Python toolbox seen in the screenshot below.

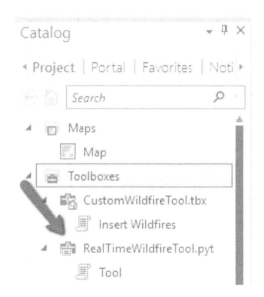

5. By default, when you right click on the toolbox and select Edit, ArcGIS Pro will automatically open your code in Notebook. To change this to the development environment of your choice. You can go to Project | Options | Geoprocessing and enter the path to your development environment as seen in the screenshot below. In this example I've provided the path to the Community Edition of PyCharm. You'll want to update this to the path specific to your environment and development environment.

6. Right click RealTimeWildfireTool.pyt and select Edit. This will open your development environment. Your development environment will vary depending upon the editor that you have defined or simply default to Notepad if you haven't defined a development environment.

7. Remember that you will not be changing the name of the class, which is Toolbox. However, you will rename the Tool class to reflect the name of the tool you want to create. Each tool will have various methods including __init__() which is the constructor for the tool along with getParameterInfo(), isLicensed(), updateParameters(), updateMessages(), and execute(). You can use the __init__() method to set initialization properties like the tool's label and description.

Look for the `Tool` class and change the name to `USGSDownload`. Also, set the `label`, and `description` as seen in the code below:

```
class USGSDownload(object):
    def __init__(self):
        """Define the tool (tool name is the name of
        the class)."""
        self.label = "USGS Download"
        self.description = "Download from USGS ArcGIS
        Server instance"
```

8. You can use the `Tool` class as a template for other tools you'd like to add to the toolbox by copying and pasting the class and it's methods. We're not going to do that in this particular exercise, but I wanted you to be aware of this. You will need to add each tool to the tools property of the `Toolbox`. Add the USGS Download tool as seen in the code below.

```
class Toolbox(object):
    def __init__(self):
        """Define the toolbox (the name of the toolbox
        is the name of the
        .pyt file)."""
        self.label = "Toolbox"
        self.alias = ""

        # List of tool classes associated with this toolbox
        self.tools = [USGSDownload]
```

9. When you close the code editor your Toolbox should automatically be refreshed. You can also manually refresh a toolbox by right clicking the toolbox and selecting Refresh.

10. You shouldn't have any errors at this time, but you can check by right clicking the toolbox and select Check Syntax.

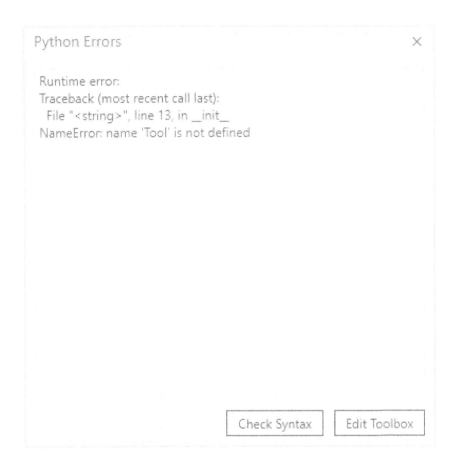

Python Errors   ✕

Runtime error:
Traceback (most recent call last):
  File "<string>", line 13, in __init__
NameError: name 'Tool' is not defined

[Check Syntax]   [Edit Toolbox]

11. Assuming that you don't have any syntax error you should see the following Toolbox/Tool structure.

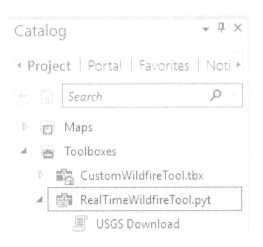

12. Almost all tools have parameters, and you set their values on the tool dialog box or within a script. When the tool is executed, the parameter values are sent to your tool's source code. Your tool reads these values and proceeds with its work. You use the `getParameterInfo()` method to define the parameters for your tool. Individual `Parameter` objects are created as part of this process. Add the following parameters in the `getParameterInfo()` method and then we'll discuss.

```
def getParameterInfo(self):
    """Define parameter definitions"""

    # First parameter
    param0 = arcpy.Parameter(
        displayName="ArcGIS Server Wildfire URL",
        name="url",
        datatype="GPString",
        parameterType="Required",
        direction="Input")
    param0.value = "https://wildfire.cr.usgs.gov/arcgis/
    rest/services/geomac_dyn/MapServer/0/query"

    # Second parameter
    param1 = arcpy.Parameter(
        displayName="Output Feature Class",
        name="out_fc",
        datatype="DEFeatureClass",
        parameterType="Required",
        direction="Input")

    params = [param0, param1]
    return params
```

13. Each `Parameter` object is created using `arcpy.Parameter` and is passed a number of arguments that define the object.
For the first `Parameter` object (`param0`) we are going to capture a URL to an ArcGIS Server map service containing current wildfire data. We give it a display name (ArcGIS Server Wildfire URL), which will be displayed on the dialog box for the tool, a name for the parameter, a data-type, parameter type (Required), and direction.

In the case of the first parameter (param0) we also assign an initial value, which is the URL to an existing map service containing wildfire data.

For the second parameter we're defining an output feature class where the wildfire data that is read from the map service will be written. An empty feature class for storing the data has already been created for you. Finally, we added both parameters to a Python list called params and return the list to the calling function

14. The main work of a tool is done inside the execute() method. This is where the geoprocessing of your tool takes place. The execute() method, seen below, can accept a number of arguments including the tool (self), parameters, and messages.

```
def execute(self, parameters, messages):
"""The source code of the tool. """
return
```

15. To access the parameter values that are passed into the tool you can use the valueAsText() method. Add the following code to access the parameter values that will be passed into your tool. Remember from a previous step that the first parameter will contain a URL to a map service containing wildfire data and the second parameter is the output feature class where the data will be written.

```
def execute(self, parameters, messages):
    inFeatures = parameters[0].valueAsText
    outFeatureClass = parameters[1].valueAsText
```

16. At this point you have created a Python toolbox, added a tool, defined the parameters for the tool, and created variables that will hold the parameter values that the end user has defined. Ultimately this tool will use the URL that is passed into the tool to connect to an ArcGIS Server map service, download the current wildfire data, and write the wildfire data to a feature class. We'll do that next.

17. Next, add the code that connects to the wildfire map service to perform a query. In this step you will also define the QueryString parameters that will be passed into the query of the map service. First we'll import the requests and json modules by adding the code below. The requests module is part of the standard conda installation associated with ArcGIS Pro. The import statements should go at the very top of your script.

```
import requests, json
```

18. Then, create the payload variable that will hold the QueryString parameters. Notice that in this case we have defined a where clause so that only fires where the

acres are greater than 5 will be returned. The `inFeatures` variable holds the URL.

```
def execute(self, parameters, messages):
    inFeatures = parameters[0].valueAsText
    outFeatureClass = parameters[1].valueAsText

    agisurl = inFeatures

    payload = { 'where': 'acres > 5','f':
        'pjson', 'outFields':
        'latitude,longitude,
        incidentname,acres'}
```

19. Submit the request to the ArcGIS Server instance and the response should be stored in a variable called `r`.

```
def execute(self, parameters, messages):
    inFeatures = parameters[0].valueAsText
    outFeatureClass = parameters[1].valueAsText

    agisurl = inFeatures

    payload = { 'where': 'acres > 5','f': 'pjson',
    'outFields': 'latitude,longitude,incidentname,acres'}

    r = requests.get(inFeatures, params=payload)
```

20. Let's test the code to make sure we're on the right track. Add the code below to your script.

```
def execute(self, parameters, messages):
    inFeatures = parameters[0].valueAsText
    outFeatureClass = parameters[1].valueAsText

    agisurl = inFeatures

    payload = { 'where': 'acres > 5','f': 'pjson',
    'outFields': 'latitude,longitude,incidentname,acres'}

    r = requests.get(inFeatures, params=payload)
    arcpy.AddMessage(r.text)
```

21. Save the file and refresh your toolbox in the Catalog pane. Execute the tool and accept the default URL. If everything is working as expected you should see a JSON object output to the progress dialog. To view the output you'll need to mouse over the message on the progress dialog. Your output will probably vary somewhat because we're pulling live data.

```
attributes : {
"latitude": 47.956760000000003,
"longitude": -113.0714,
"incidentname": "Scalp",
"acres": 11425
},
"geometry": {
"x": -12587052.147068366,
"y": 6099665.3530677725
}
},
{
"attributes": {
"latitude": 46.004620000000003,
"longitude": -114.7846,
"incidentname": "Crow 2",
"acres": 748
},
"geometry": {
"x": -12777764.69096761,
"y": 5781090.6178344972
}
}
```

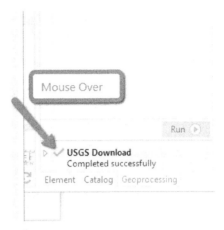

22. Return to the execute() method and convert the JSON object to a Python dictionary. Also, comment out the arcpy.AddMessage() function call you implemented in the last step.

```python
def execute(self, parameters, messages):
    inFeatures = parameters[0].valueAsText
    outFeatureClass = parameters[1].valueAsText

    agisurl = inFeatures

    payload = { 'where': 'acres > 5','f': 'pjson',
    'outFields': 'latitude,longitude,incidentname,acres'}

    r = requests.get(inFeatures, params=payload)


    #arcpy.AddMessage(r.text)
    decoded = json.loads(r.text)
```

23. Create an `InsertCursor` by passing in the output feature class defined in the tool dialog along with the fields that will be populated. We then start a `for` loop that loops through each of the features (wildfires) that have been returned from the request to the ArcGIS Server map service. The decoded variable is a Python dictionary. Inside the `for` loop we retrieve the `incidentname`, `latitude`, `longitude`, `acres` from the `attributes` dictionary. Finally, we call the `insertRow()` method to insert a new row into the feature class along with the fire name and acres as attributes. Progress information is written to the Progress Dialog and the counter is updated.

```python
def execute(self, parameters, messages):
    inFeatures = parameters[0].valueAsText
    outFeatureClass = parameters[1].valueAsText

    agisurl = inFeatures

    payload = { 'where': 'acres > 5','f': 'pjson',
    'outFields': 'latitude,longitude,incidentname,acres'}

    r = requests.get(inFeatures, params=payload)

    decoded = json.loads(r.text)

    with arcpy.da.InsertCursor(outFeatureClass,
    ("SHAPE@XY", "NAME", "ACRES")) as cur:
        cntr = 1
        for rslt in decoded['features']:
            fireName = rslt['attributes']['incidentname']
            latitude = rslt['attributes']['latitude']
            longitude = rslt['attributes']['longitude']
            acres = rslt['attributes']['acres']

            cur.insertRow([(longitude,latitude),
            fireName, acres])
    arcpy.AddMessage("Record number: " + str(cntr) + "
    written to feature class")
```

24. You can check your code against a solution file found at `c:\Student\ProgrammingPro\Solutions\Scripts\RealTimeWildfireTool.py`.

25. Save the file and refresh your Python toolbox

26. Double click the **USGS Download** tool.

27. Leave the default URL and select the **RealTimeFires** feature class in the **WildlandFires** geodatabase. The **RealTimeFires** feature class is empty and has fields for NAME and ACRES.

28. Click **OK** to execute the tool. The number of features written to the feature class will vary depending upon the current wildfire activity. Remember that this tool is pulling real time data from a USGS map service. Most of the time there is at least a little activity but it is possible (but not likely) that there wouldn't be any wildfires in the U.S. depending upon the time of year you run the tool.

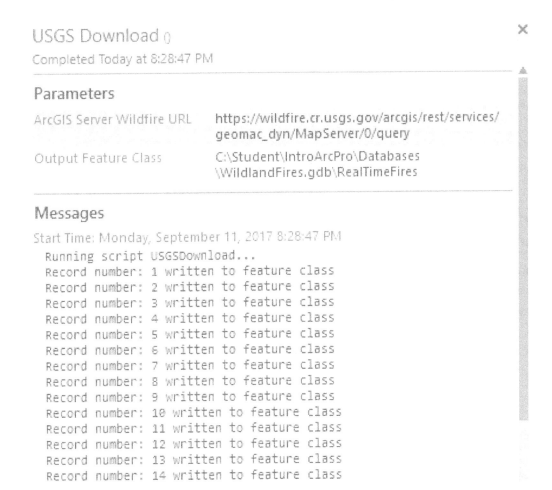

USGS Download ()   ✕

Completed Today at 8:28:47 PM

Parameters

ArcGIS Server Wildfire URL   https://wildfire.cr.usgs.gov/arcgis/rest/services/
                                  geomac_dyn/MapServer/0/query

Output Feature Class   C:\Student\IntroArcPro\Databases
                                  \WildlandFires.gdb\RealTimeFires

Messages

Start Time: Monday, September 11, 2017 8:28:47 PM
  Running script USGSDownload...
  Record number: 1 written to feature class
  Record number: 2 written to feature class
  Record number: 3 written to feature class
  Record number: 4 written to feature class
  Record number: 5 written to feature class
  Record number: 6 written to feature class
  Record number: 7 written to feature class
  Record number: 8 written to feature class
  Record number: 9 written to feature class
  Record number: 10 written to feature class
  Record number: 11 written to feature class
  Record number: 12 written to feature class
  Record number: 13 written to feature class
  Record number: 14 written to feature class

29. View the feature class in ArcGIS Pro to see the features. Your output will vary since this is real-time wildfire data.

In conclusion...

Python toolboxes provide a new way of creating custom geoprocessing tools. The creation of these tools, including the definition of parameters, validation, and execution is encapsulated into a single Python script.

Made in the USA
Monee, IL
05 November 2019